...

"

Cook
. She
e-age

y way
—you

nd let
—with
oals
f her

irley
er as
ove-
did,
s of

BUILDING on the BACK FORTY

A humorous, helpful look at life after 40.

SHIRLEY COOK

ACCENT BOOKS
Denver, Colorado

MEMBER OF
EVANGELICAL CHRISTIAN
PUBLISHERS ASSOCIATION

ACCENT BOOKS
12100 W. Sixth Avenue
P.O. Box 15337
Denver, Colorado 80215

Copyright © 1978 Accent-B/P Publications
Printed in United States of America

Library of Congress Catalog Card Number: 78-53324

ISBN 0-89636-003-2

*To the love of my life
who gives his support
and calls me his wife:
my husband, Les.*

Contents

Prologue

Many books focusing
on *CHANGE* are finding their way onto the list
of best-sellers. There are books describing
the way to change your outlook, your avocation,
your lifestyle, and even your mother-in-law.
Several of the most recent books deal with
changes that come uninvited into the middle life,
and have been tagged the "better than ever"
years or the "mid-life crisis." Many of us passing
through this stage of our lives agree with the current
authors that there are problems that often seem
insurmountable.
I, too, was plunged into these years, surprised and
bewildered at first, and only slightly comforted by
the knowledge that others had passed this way
before me.
Yes, there certainly is an adjustment to be made in
the middle years, an adjustment to the middle-age
mopes. And, like my peers, I have an opinion to
offer—one with a different viewpoint. I see life
as a great open countryside, virgin territory waiting
to be cultivated.
I think back to those early days when our fore-
fathers settled our land and gave us a fertile and
productive heritage. Their property, often consisting

of 160 acres, was divided into parcels of forty acres each. That section on which they built their homes and planted their crops became known as the "south forty." There they lived, loved, learned and sometimes lost. Yet they knew there was always more land—fallow, uncultivated land, the back forty.

This term, the back forty, is still used by farmers and ranchers today in designating the back section of their acreage. However, with our large population, that portion is seldom left uncultivated, but is wisely used, rotating crops for the greatest yield.

I use the expression, "building on the back forty," to visualize the after-forty years—those years in the back section of life which await cultivation and a rich harvest.

Up to this time, I have married, given birth and raised a family of six children. Now I look ahead, admittedly with some qualms, to those years when my life takes a new direction. With my family almost grown, my husband successful and fulfilled through his work, I find myself on the edge of a new territory, one where I may grow into my full potential as a woman, a Christian, a person.

This adventure is by no means limited to those in their forties. Some reach this stage of life earlier, and some, struggling through the forties and fifties, may even now begin building on their back forty.

So—come on along. Don't think about age. Think instead about change—change for the better on the back forty.

Les and Shirley Cook of
Stockton, California, look
to their future with a spirit
of adventure.

1

Surveying the Land

It all began on my forty-first birthday. Until then I had thought of age as an inconsequential fact of life. I hadn't, like some of my friends, fallen apart at the sight of thirty candles on my birthday cake. And chasing children kept me too busy to notice when thirty-five rolled around.

I admit that reaching forty excited me, but only because I had heard that, "Life begins at forty." And after twenty-one years of marriage and six children, I could use a fresh beginning. But the fortieth year galloped by like every other, leaving me in the dust on a downhill track. So I gritted my teeth and dug in my heels.

No matter how many well-wishers called or brought gifts, the tears clung just inside my eyelids, ready to spill over at any moment. Even a night out with the man in my life didn't help.

"Honey," I whispered between the salad and the soup, "I have to talk to you about something— something important to me."

He wiped his mouth and leaned across the table, his eyes fixed on my face.

"I'm middle-aged," I gulped, "and it's awful."

Was that the flicker of candlelight in his eye, or was he going to laugh?

"Honestly, I'm on my way downhill, and I don't feel like I've ever lived—you know, really lived."

It wasn't the candlelight. He began to laugh.

"You're not middle-aged," he said, dabbing at his eyes. "I'm five years older than you, and I'm sure not middle-aged." He poked at a limp lettuce leaf. "You just need some new interests now that you have more time on your hands," he said, turning his attention to the relish dish.

"Hmm, well, I don't know. Maybe."

I thought about his words as I choked down the rest of my dinner. They just didn't coincide with what I had seen that morning when I stepped out of the shower.

I had turned and faced the full-length mirror. That was a middle-aged mirror if I ever saw one. Its chin drooped. In fact, almost everything under the chin, down to the ankles, drooped. And what didn't droop, bulged. I was at least twenty pounds overweight.

"Well," I comforted myself, "it's inevitable after six babies to sport a few leftover lumps and bumps."

I then turned to the vanity mirror. Just look at that hair. Blah! Dull and lifeless. And the few gray hairs poking through unwired my already limp ego. Why, I even found a couple of gray eyebrow hairs!

Then, stretching my neck closer to the mirror, I noticed some new wrinkles around my eyes and mouth. (Had they been there yesterday?) And what were those funny lines on my throat? Was that what was called "turkey neck"? Horrors. My skin was dry. My hair was dry. I was dry.

And each day passed drier and more ho-hum than

Horrors! Is that what is called "turkey neck"?

the day before, with the children needing less and less of my attention. Only three at home now, and they would soon leave the nest, their own wings strong enough to support them. Would I become *passé*? Obsolete?

As we buzzed down the highway in our little yellow Opel, I felt miserable (some birthday) and hardly spoke on the ride home. I had to work these things out in my own mind. So, after kissing my husband goodnight, I retreated to the family room where I could snuggle down into a comfortable chair, sneak a few high calorie snacks and struggle through my middle-age mopes.

Out of habit, I picked up my Bible and opened it to the New Testament. First Corinthians 6:19, 20 caught my eye.

"What? know ye not that your body is the temple of the Holy Ghost which is in you, which ye have of God, and ye are not your own? For ye are bought with a price: therefore glorify God in your body, and in your spirit, which are God's."

I had read that verse many times. Even underlined it. But tonight the words stood out in bold print. *My body . . . His temple.*

I had let God's temple fall into disrepair. I hadn't taken care of my body. I was overweight and out of condition. And my spirit was defeated, too. I was thinking the same old thoughts. My body was growing, but my mind wasn't.

As I sat there in the quiet, the Lord began to show me the possibility of building a temple that would honor Him. It would be a joint effort, not an ordinary self-improvement project. God Himself would be my partner.

"For we are labourers together with God: ye are

God's husbandry, ye are God's building" (I Corinthians 3:9).

That building project started several years ago, and there's still much to be done. But this book tells how I am growing into a happier, more fulfilled woman, and is written with the hope of encouraging others going through the middle-age mopes to begin building a new house, too.

As I build, I find the years ahead are no longer threatening, but thrilling. And now I'm convinced that the years after forty can and should be the very best.

So whether you're forty-one or sixty-one, stop and survey the land, the back forty. Where are you right now? Are you satisfied with yourself? Is God satisfied with His temple?

If not, then read on.

2

Choosing a Floor Plan

"Do I have any clean undershirts?" my husband called from the bathroom, his voice slightly crisp.

"Mom, where's my blue sock? One's been missing for ages."

"Hey," shrieked another daughter from behind the refrigerator door, "there's no milk for my Cheerios. How can I eat?"

Oh, no, what else could go wrong so early in the day? Just then, the baby of the family charged into the kitchen waving a dog-eared note from her teacher, "Mom, I forgot to tell you. I *have* to bring twenty-four cupcakes to school today."

After pulling an undershirt out of the dryer, a blue sock dangling from its armhole, pointing out that some people eat eggs instead of cereal for breakfast, and promising to have cupcakes at school before noon, I remembered my decision of the night before. There would be some changes made. And one would be to organize my time better.

I already had an endless list banging around inside my head, but where should I start? And how could I possibly change all those things in my remaining lifetime? I had to have a plan of some kind. That's why I was in such a mess now. I had let my life just happen instead of directing it myself—or better, letting God direct it.

I was sure many others had been through similar problems and had written some books on the subject. In fact, I had even read a few.

Two different Christian books told me how to become more of a woman; but one left me unfastened, and the other, totalled. I had finally decided they were written for younger or less inhibited women than I.

Somehow I just couldn't bring myself to stomp my foot and shake my saucy curls to show my anger. And dressing up in a different costume every night had proven a disaster. All I could find were some old Halloween costumes: a cat, a clown and a Donald Duck—more of a woman?

For those of a personality unlike mine, more power to them, but I needed a different angle.

That's how I found myself in the neighborhood mall browsing through the bookstore for a new answer to an old question—how to change for the better in my after-forty years.

I loved the heady fragrance of the freshly inked pages, and the brightly colored jackets cried out for me to hold them. Several of the displayed best-sellers on self-improvement had already squeezed themselves into a place on my bookshelves; but I had experienced little success in either intimidation or assertiveness.

Books covering those topics had been studied several months before as I looked for a fuller understanding of myself and better communication with my husband. But instead of the desired results, *he* was assertive and *I* was intimidated. Foiled again.

Giving up on those self-help suggestions, once more I had settled down into the middle-age mopes with my bleak future, known only to God, lingering behind each new birthday cake.

Known only to God?

That was it. Why should I look around in a bookstore for the answer? I had a Book right at home that had all the answers. The Lord would show me through His Word how to build a temple to His specifications. And He wouldn't expect it to happen all at once. Patience and strength would be given as I needed it.

"I can do all things through Christ which strengtheneth me," says Philippians 4:13.

Driving back home, I tingled with excitement at the prospect of finding the right floor plan—His plan—for my new building project.

And I knew His plan could be adjusted to fit my own particular needs. Since each of us is different, God, who knows and loves those differences, leads us in distinctly personal ways.

Just think—my own floor plan. An original design. As some of my old house was still in good condition, I had to be careful not to remodel things better left unchanged. I would analyze my situation, then draw up a blueprint of the plan He showed me.

So, pen in hand, Bible open before me, and a mirror propped up on the table, I became a designing woman.

What were the most obvious changes I should make? What could be done to improve family relationships? What did I like or dislike about myself?

The task ahead seemed awesome, and I felt like throwing in the pen, but my Partner kept prodding me along with images of the new me.

That's when I bowed my head and prayed, *Lord, You know how frustrated I feel. I really want my life to be better from now on. But, honestly, I just don't know where to begin, or how to go about it. Please show me how to build on my back forty.*

3

Drawing
the Blueprints

I glanced up and saw myself staring back from the mirror. That same face had been looking at me for years, but lately it had a tired, drawn look (if round cheeks can look drawn, that is). Was it just my age that made me look that way or was it something deeper, even more serious, than the middle-age mopes? I'd think about that later.

Right now I wanted to get down some tangible changes to be made. Some building blueprints for my back forty.

The outer structure was my first concern. That's what I could see, and unfortunately, what everyone else had to look at, too.

So I would start with the body. After all, when a house is built, the work begins, not on the interior, but on the framework. But what kind of house did I want? What did God want?

My old model wasn't exactly Early American, but more the rambling ranch style—spread out. Since I didn't need that much room to rattle around in anymore, I decided on a slim, sleek building. A house that was attractive, yet compact.

That meant not only a diet to shed all those excess pounds, but also an exercise plan to tighten and firm up flabby muscles. So I wrote *DIET* and *EXERCISE* at the top of my list.

Then, there was my hair. My dry, unruly hair. Back-combing and harsh sprays were no longer "in." Such treatment had dried and damaged my hair, not to mention dating me as a practically pre-historic person.

And there were those oft-repeated words of my husband, "I like hair that's soft to touch, not hair I skin my knuckles on." So I knew he'd be glad for me to get rid of my "helmet hair."

How about the color? I wasn't too excited about gray hair. None of the women in my family had it. Even my eighty-nine-year-old grandmother keeps hers a soft ash brown.

I had tried many color combinations, but couldn't make up my mind. I was usually a frosty blonde in the summer and a warm brunette in the winter. My husband had even been teased about having a girl-friend, but it was only me in my bottled bouffant. Not sure what I would do yet, I wrote next to Number 2: *CHANGE HAIRSTYLE.*

There really wasn't much I could do with the area under my hairstyle. I knew my husband would never go for a facelift—for either one of us. But there *were* some things I could change. The pale pink lipstick and frosty blue eyeshadow only exaggerated the lines that could use a good moisturizer. My eyebrows would look better with some thinning—those gray ones would have to go. And, well, Item 3 became *FACE.*

Putting down my pen, I noticed my hands. Hmm. I

hadn't really looked at them in years. They'd always been so busy wringing diapers, wiping tears and working in the garden. They were good hands. Strong hands. I had never been accused of having a dead fish handshake. But they were dry and red. My nails were uneven and stubby. I would so something about my hands, too. That would be Number 4 on my blueprint.

I sat back and crossed my legs. They didn't cross too well. "Heavy thighs," I had often said, "are the result of my German background." But I knew they would slim down as I lost weight; and I could find some exercises to firm them up so I wouldn't be accused of wearing baggy nylons.

The general structure of my body and face couldn't be changed. I would always be long-waisted and short-legged, long-necked and thin-lipped. But my blueprint would be like an accountant's well-ordered books. The assets as well as the liabilities would be taken into consideration, and hopefully, the end results would be well balanced.

After finishing the outside plans, I turned my attention to the rooms inside my temple. Of course, there would be a living room where I would entertain and fellowship with others. That needed a lot of work, for I had neglected reaching out to others to draw them into God's forever family—a family where there is room for living and growing.

From the living room would be an entrance to the kitchen, a place of warmth and comfort. Good meals served with love, as well as spiritual food for me and my family would be prepared there.

Opening off the kitchen, I would have a family room where we could get together for fun and conversation. Each person's interests could be pursued there; and I would try to find a new interest for myself, too.

Toward the back of the house, overlooking the garden, would be the bedroom. It would symbolize a special place of love and closeness between me and my husband. I hated to admit that I had erected some walls between us, but our new bedroom would be entirely different. I would decorate our marriage with fresh love and excitement. Whee, I could hardly wait to start.

I wanted another room in my new home. A closet. It would be a small, but very important room. My former closet had become cluttered with the old clothes of self-righteousness and some long-forgotten sins. But I planned to get rid of those things, and keep my new closet as a secret meeting place with the Owner of my house.

Well, that about finished my blueprint. I knew I could make some changes along the way, or even add some rooms, as I saw need. But, at least now I had something to work from. A beginning. A blueprint for the back forty.

4

Counting the Cost

As I looked over my blueprint, the years ahead took on new excitement. I *could* do it. I knew I could. Through Christ, I can do all things—even change for the better after cresting that hill posted 40.

Thinking about it made me so happy, I got up and fixed myself a heaping bowl of ice cream.

"Mom," piped my middle daughter, "I thought you were on a diet."

"I'm starting soon," I sputtered. "After I've done some planning and . . ."

Whoops, I was making excuses. I couldn't keep that up while building on my back forty. So I decided then and there to carry out my project without telling *everyone* what I was doing. That way, they wouldn't feel responsibile for keeping me in line, and I wouldn't have to make excuses when I failed. And I knew, from past experiences, there would be occasional failures.

After hiding my blueprint, I began to go over the list again in my head. *Diet, exercise, hairstyle . . .*

"Do you want some make-up for dinner?" I asked

"Do you want some make-up for dinner?"

my husband as he walked through the kitchen.

"Some what?" he blurted, eyeing me with cat-like curiosity.

"I said, do you want some—a—a . . ."

"I heard what you said. What did you mean—make-up?"

I smiled what I hoped was a cute pixieish grin, and mumbled, "Uh, I was thinking I'd make up—a—make up some cookies. Yes, would you like some cookies later?"

"Yeah, sure," he said, scratching his head as he sauntered out of the room.

I hadn't planned to spend the evening baking, but as I did, I mulled over the various changes and plans I had considered that afternoon. My blueprint wasn't clear enough. I had to make a more detailed list. (Oh, joy, I love making lists.) One that would project the cost in time and effort, and could be checked off as I completed each item.

I was an old hand at itemizing things—anything. I had lists of people to call, places to go and projects to start. I listed everything from "Christmas cookies to bake," to "Easter eggs to hide." I even had lists listing the categories of my lists. My children's names listed in alphabetical order was only one example proving the usefulness of my lists. At dinnertime, I just poked my head out the door and hollered, "Time to eat, two B's, C, D, G and K!" A great time-saver.

Yes, I'd work over my list a little more. So, that evening when the two B's and C had gone to bed, and L, my husband, had retired to the living room to absorb some culture via the stereo and a library book, I retrieved my blueprint from the bottom drawer of the desk.

Not that I was hiding anything, but it would be fun to build slowly, but surely, on my back forty and watch the reactions of people when the work was done. Like those pre-fab jobs that go up over night.

They'd be amazed. "Oh, whatever have you done to become so beautiful, so charming and so lovable?"

I'd smile mysteriously and swoop by, leaving everyone gawking after me.

But was that what I wanted? Attention for myself?

No. That (self) was part of my problem. No sense adding to the frustration. Besides, wasn't my whole purpose in starting this new work to honor God in this temple I call *"Me"*?

As a Christian for over twenty years, Christ is real to me. I have the assurance of eternal life and a purpose for living. But, somehow, in the everyday business of *being,* I had begun directing my own affairs from the sidelines until, little by little, I had taken over and shoved Christ out of the central place in His temple.

But I wanted to change all that. For Him to be the Lord of my life and abide in me and I in Him, I realized, would cost me something. My selfish motives would have to go. I could no longer be *Number One.*

I wondered if the cost was too great. No—I wasn't satisfied with my life the way it was, and it certainly wouldn't improve without some effort. So, having compared the cost of continuing on the south forty with building on my back forty, I was certain it was worth it—whatever the price.

On with the show.

5

Laying
the Foundation

It was finally time to begin the work. I had drawn up the blueprints, counted the cost, and was past procrastination. What should go up first? The framework? The roof? I had seen enough building projects around town to know that the foundation was the first, and possibly the most important, part. If the foundation were weak, the entire building would be weak.

But ever since the night of my forty-first birthday when God showed me the possibility of changing for the better in my after-forty years, I had felt a struggle deep down inside—a weakness I didn't want to face.

I wanted my life to be more worthwhile and satisfying, yet I knew that if it were up to me, it would be nothing more than a short-term project. It would last a month or two, then slowly sift down into the sand on which it was built. Then I realized that God expected not just a partnership, but full control—Owner, Contractor and Foreman. My reluctance to turn the entire project over to Him was the cause of my struggle.

About that time, a little booklet "happened" to fall into my hands. In it were pictures of circles illustrating the lives of the natural man, one who does not know Christ as Lord and Saviour; the spiritual man, one who allows Christ to control the whole life; and the carnal man, the Christian who insists on running his own life.

I could clearly see that I was in the last group—knowing and loving Jesus Christ, yet not surrendered to the direction of the Holy Spirit. I was a carnal Christian.

My interests and plans were confused and without harmony just as the carnal circle showed. And as long as I insisted on being the contractor of my building project, the results would continue along the lines of confusion and clutter.

I wanted a life that would make me a completely whole person. I wanted a life that would minister to the needs of others. And above all, I wanted a life that would honor God. And according to Jesus' words in John 10:10, the only solution was a total commitment to Him. "I am come that they might have life, and that they might have it more abundantly."

So, that day in the solitude of my room, I bowed down in prayer asking God, the Holy Spirit, to take over in my life as Lord. I confessed my sins of unbelief and rebellion, and some others I'd rather not mention. Then, on the basis of the Word of God, I believed that He had heard me and had kept His promise to fill me with His Holy Spirit.

I didn't have an emotional experience, only peace and joy. I *did* have the assurance that, "if we ask anything according to his will, he heareth us: And if we know that he hear us, whatsoever we ask, we know that we have the petitions that we desired of him" (I John 5:14,15).

And I was certain of His will for every one of His children to be filled with the Holy Spirit, for in Ephesians 5:18, He commands it: "be not drunk with wine . . . but be filled with the Spirit."

So if you, too, have come along this far and have made a decision to build on your back forty, stop—be sure your foundation is strong. "For other foundation can no man lay than that is laid, which is Jesus Christ" (I Corinthians 3:11). Does He have the final say in your plans?

After settling that, I glanced over my blueprints again. Wow, had I drawn up a skyscraper instead of a little bungalow?

One more look in the full-length mirror. The droops and bulges were still there. The hairstyle was still blah, and waiting for a miracle were the wrinkles and dry skin. But there was a sparkle in my eyes that hadn't been there before. It seemed to shine out from someplace within my spirit, reminding me that I was about to begin a successful new adventure. A building on the back forty.

6

Starting to Build

Sunday, Monday, Tuesday, Dietday—time to start building. I had always begun my diets on Monday morning, but this time was different. The emphasis was on one meal at a time instead of one day or week at a time.

While making up my blueprint for the back forty, I had planned a diet strategy. I wouldn't fail this time. I determined to stick with it until I reached my desired weight of 120 pounds, and I wouldn't suffer either. Why? Because eating plenty, pleasantly and purposefully, I had to succeed. I had learned my lesson well. No more crash or fad diets for me.

I remember one day as I suffered through a self-imposed famine, my husband had asked, "Why are you always sucking on something?" He had pointed to my face and added, "It looks like you're always eating, but you're getting downright gaunt through the face."

"Well, thanks a lot," I said, trying not to cry.

Why did I feel so depressed all the time? I should be

happy, losing about five pounds a week, but I felt terrible.

"I'm not always eating. See," I stuck out my tongue, "it's only a prune pit."

"A prune pit! You mean that's what you're always sucking on?"

"Yes," I answered, pulling in my cheeks. "This new diet allows three prunes a day, along with raw vegetables and one serving of meat. Sucking the pits is supposed to cut down my appetite."

"It just makes you look dopey," he responded with a smile. "Like a squirrel who doesn't know where to hide its acorn." As he reached out to me, I ran from the room crying.

That night I began to eat normally (for me) again, and had soon regained the weight I had lost, plus a few extra pounds. But, in eating more, my formerly cheery disposition had returned. So much for prune pits.

Then—there was the candy diet. The directions said that two before each meal would satisfy the appetite, but they were so good, I ended up eating them all day, and not only gained four pounds, but four cavities as well.

Through the years, I've tried over-the-counter pills (which did absolutely nothing except make a dent in my grocery budget), under-the-counter capsules (which made me the life of the party), and across-the-counter chewing gum (which I accidentally confused with a stimulant to regularity one sleepy-eyed morning).

I ate grapefruit until my lips and eyes took on a continual pucker, and drank blended eggs and orange juice until my skin had a bright glow—a yellow one. Every fad diet ended with me depressed, discouraged and several pounds heavier.

This time I prayed about it. "If any of you lack wisdom, let him ask of God, that giveth to all men liberally, and upbraideth not; and it shall be given him" (James 1:5). What was God's plan for a healthful and effective weight loss for *me?*

Since I had possibly injured my health with crash diets, I felt God's leading to go see my doctor for a checkup before beginning any construction on my back forty.

After a thorough examination, he smiled that reassuring smile I had been waiting for and said, "You're in good physical condition, except for that twenty extra pounds you're carrying."

Twenty pounds. It was like trying to hide two big sacks of potatoes and not doing a very good job of it. And since I had added a potato at a time, it would have to come off the same way. Could I last that long?

"But how can I get rid of it?" I whined. "I've tried everything, and all I get is depressed and cranky."

"That's because you're too impatient," he said. "Losing weight wisely and keeping it off takes time and effort." He leaned back in his chair and removed his glasses. "Are you willing to pay the price?"

I remembered that I had decided building on my back forty was worthwhile, whatever the cost.

"Y-yes," I stammered, wondering if by "price" he meant I would get a huge bill at the end of the month.

"All right then, here is a sensible diet for you to follow. It's identical to the one used by a well-known diet organization. If you enjoy doing things with a group, I suggest you join them. If not, you can buy their cookbook on any bookstand. Trying new recipes may give you the challenge you need to continue with it."

He said I didn't have to count calories as they were figured into the diet. I would lose about two pounds a week. (I guess you could say I was eating for two!) And if I followed it consistently, I would lose the entire twenty pounds without great suffering, for myself or my family.

"And, as an added benefit," he said, "the new eating habits you learn will assure you of good health in the years ahead." My back forty years.

I breezed out of his office, the diet in my hand, the Holy Spirit in my heart and a creed for my project—"Being confident of this very thing, that he which hath begun a good work in you will perform it until the day of Jesus Christ" (Philippians 1:6).

7

Gathering More Tools

I wish I could say that every board and brick fit perfectly into place the first time, but problems arise in diets and in building projects, no matter how well planned. And I began to meet with opposition right from the beginning.

Friends and family said I wasn't eating enough (and I was inclined to agree), because I finished so quickly. Those accustomed TV snacks weren't on my diet, and I felt left out as the family munched their way through "Monday Night at the Movies." And to top it all, the dial on the scale sometimes didn't move for days. Surely a day's deprivation deserved a down-moving dial!

Needing more tools to help me get my temple into shape, I discovered four things that really helped me. First, I began to eat more slowly. That sounds easy, but it wasn't. Just as it took many years to learn how to consume enough for three in the time it takes one to finish a meal, I now had to unlearn that bad habit and begin spending the time it would take one person to eat three meals. Why?

Several reasons. The most obvious was that if I ate more slowly, I wouldn't eat as much—unless I planned to spend the day at the table. But the primary motive for taking longer (the experts say at least twenty minutes) is that it gives the food time to be converted into blood sugar, signaling the brain that I'm satisfied. And when I'm satisfied, I don't keep looking for something else to put into my mouth—for those unnecessary calories slip quickly over the lips, through the stomach and onto the hips! Sometimes I even set the timer—twenty minutes.

Slowing down was hard at first, especially since I was used to cleaning my plate and the children's leftovers before the six o'clock news. But I found I could eat more slowly by deliberately putting my fork down after each bite and carefully chewing every morsel. I enjoyed my meal much more and was surprised at how satisfied and full I felt on half of what I had previously eaten.

Tool Number 2: When eating anything, I always sat in my regular place at the table. This dicouraged wolfing cookie dough at the counter and slices of bologna while making lunches. (Are there really calories in the food you eat while standing?)

This new practice eliminated indiscriminate eating in front of the TV or while curled up with a good book. In fact, I found it a good idea just to leave my book on the sofa and turn my back to the TV, because indulging in other activities while eating seemed to erase all consciousness of having eaten, and the hunger remained as intense as ever. There may be exceptions to this sitting-in-my-regular-place rule, however—like the night my husband's clients came home for after-the-concert refreshments. I had prepared a dessert that was attractive as well as

Sitting alone at my regular place, I chewed and concentrated on the taste.

acceptable on my diet, and after serving it, I excused myself and went back to the kitchen.

Sitting alone at the table in my regular place, I chewed, set down my fork, and concentrated on the taste. After about fifteen minutes, my husband, followed by our bewildered guests, wandered into the kitchen to see what had happened to me. You know, they've never accepted another invitation!

Practicing both these helps until they became natural took time, but now I use them whenever possible and practical as genuine tools in my building program.

Two more tools were great helps—keeping a diary and weighing only once a week.

I bought a small spiral notebook to keep near the table and wrote down what, when and why I ate. What an eye-opener! I thought a few cookies now and then, plus a dish of ice cream or a handful of peanuts wouldn't matter, so I didn't bother to record them. But even if they didn't show up on the pages of my diary, they *did* show up on the posterier of my *derriere*.

I also learned from my diary entries that I often ate out of boredom or anxiety, rather than hunger. Knowing this, I could make plans to become involved in something else, such as working outside in the garden or taking a walk. Anything but hanging around the kitchen!

However, my plans occasionally backfired. Example: One gloomy day when the trees were veiled with fog and the birds clung to the branches like full-blown pussy willows, I shivered at the thought of the cold dampness that would follow me on a walk, so decided instead to take on an indoor project. Our bathroom needed painting, and there in the garage was some green enamel.

It took two days to finish, and ended up looking like a hallway in a government building. But after another week of repainting and papering, we were finally able to enter without getting sick. At least I stayed on my diet—I was too busy to think about eating between meals.

Tool Number 4: Weighing only once a week was probably the hardest change of all. I suppose most compulsive eaters and dieters are like me in that we weigh too often. I weighed first thing in the morning, right after lunch, and before bedtime. I realized it had become an obsession when my husband refused to let me bring the bathroom scale on our weekend back-packing trip.

But I think the best reason for not weighing every day is that it's too discouraging. Feeling proud and perhaps a little deprived for not indulging in a hot fudge sundae when out with the girls, I would get on the scale next day, and find to my surprise that the dial seemed stuck.

"Phooey, why suffer?" I would cry. "Today I'll eat anything and everything I want."

But if I could just hold out a few days, I would see a difference. I once read that, to shed one pound, a dieter must eat 3,500 fewer calories than the body uses. My diet is constructed to enable me to lose two pounds a week—that's 7,000 calories a week less than I usually eat, or 1,000 fewer calories a day. Just think, I ate that many extra calories to add those unwanted pounds, too.

By weighing only once a week instead of every day I could actually see the numbers getting smaller, and felt greatly encouraged to continue.

These are some of the major habit changes that I

made while dieting, and hope you find them helpful while remodeling your temple, too.

And you know what? In controlling my appetite for food, I discovered that I have more of an appetite for the spiritual nourishment in the Word of God— and that can only do me good.

Jesus said, "I am the bread of life: he that cometh to me shall never hunger; and he that believeth on me shall never thirst" (John 6:35).

Lord, give me this day my daily bread.

8

Paying the Laborer

Pay Day! Every hard worker not only looks forward to it, but deserves it. And builders on the back forty are no different. We like rewards, too— some tangible recognition for our successful endeavors. Since I had decided not to burden my family with, "Oh, I lost two pounds this week," or "Boo hoo, I only lost a half pound this week," I had no one to pat me on the back except myself.

Oh, I knew that the ultimate reward for my diet would come eventually—a healthier, more attractive body. But, unlike my crash diets, this one was slow. It would take weeks to see a difference, and as a basically impatient person (I peek at Christmas gifts), I felt I needed some kind of prize that I could see—*NOW*.

My first thought was to treat myself to a hot fudge sundae every time I lost two pounds. But even *I* realized the self-defeating aspect of such wages. Then I remembered how Margaret had worked out her reward system.

Every time she lost five pounds she raced to the store to buy some extravagance she wouldn't ordinarily consider—like a black negligee, or an ounce of her favorite perfume. Her plan worked well at first, until she developed an unquenchable desire for extras that went on long after she had reached her goal. She was totally frustrated, trying to decide whether to give up the presents or continue dieting until she was too thin to wear her new clothes, when her husband stepped in and put his foot down—on her credit card.

Then another friend, Betty, needing fortification, adopted a monthly eat-at-your-favorite-restaurant plan. She loved dressing up to go out with her husband, and found the night out added *only* to her self esteem and not to her weight. That plan may work for you, too. Once a month, eating different food in a different place (but still in control) may be just the incentive you need. But each of us has to decide what, if any, prize we want to give ourselves.

The reward system is nothing new. Even a well-known diet organization gives rewards—lovely diamond-studded pins to those who reach their goals.

But, as I said, I'm impatient and waiting until I had lost all my unwanted poundage, or waiting until the end of the month for a dinner out, or even waiting until I had lost two pounds just didn't satisfy me. So here's how I solved my problem.

As I mentioned before, I kept a daily record of what, when and why I ate, and at the end of each day I curled up in my favorite chair and appraised my entry for the day. If I had kept within my diet 100 percent, I put one dollar in my empty Swiss Mocha can. If not, I took a dollar out.

At first, I did a lot of exchanging—out of the can, into the grocery money; then out of the grocery

If I had kept within my diet 100 percent, I put
one dollar in the can. If not . . .

money back into the can. The clerks at the store eyed me suspiciously as I handed them dollar bills dusted with tiny granules of Swiss Mocha. Anyway, I soon learned it was to my advantage to stay with the diet long enough to build up my reserve, as well as lose weight on a consistent basis.

And as my cash reserve began to build, so did my willpower. I found that staying on my diet all day, every day, wasn't as difficult as I had thought it would be.

Then came the fun time, deciding what to buy with my "earnings." I wouldn't buy milk or bread to replenish the larder, nor would I spend my hard-earned cash on new shoes for the children. That money was *mine* to splurge—maybe for those gold slippers, or some of that new bronze blusher. I had many ideas, ideas that kept me working at my diet and filling up my little tin can.

Of course, the dollar-a-day plan is only a short-term reward system, like the stars given to Sunday School students for saying one Bible verse. But, after learning a specified list of verses, they usually receive another, more substantial award. And so will I. There's nothing wrong with working for rewards, and it *does* encourage consistency.

Even God rewards His children for work well done. He promises a prize for running the race of life well (I Corinthians 9:24); an incorruptible crown for mastering the body (I Corinthians 9:25); a crown of righteousness for those who love His appearing (II Timothy 4:8); and many others. He knows our need for tangible proof—proof confirmed in His Word—of these rewards which will be ours in Heaven.

But, for the Christian, there is another short-term reward that comes even more often than the dollar-a-day plan I developed. And, although intangible, this reward can be felt. It is the sense of joy in pleasing the Lord through the act of moderation. Whenever a child of God acts in obedience to His Word, he is blessed with a sense of peace and joy welling up within the spirit. Now is there any reward that begins to compare to the joy of unbroken fellowship with the God of Heaven?

But, just as the greatest rewards come at the end of a Christian's life when we hear Jesus say, "Well done, good and faithful servant; . . . enter thou into the joy of thy lord" (Matthew 25:23), so the best and most lasting rewards come at the end of the dieter's struggle. Whether it be a diamond pin or a new Size 8 pantsuit, it is something to work toward.

Of course, there are those strong-willed people who finish anything and everything they set their minds to. They keep their New Year's resolutions, wash on Monday, iron on Tuesday, and always stay within their budgets. That's great. They won't need to ply themselves with rewards to continue building on their back forty.

But, for every one of them, there are ten of us who, although we have good intentions and proper motivation, are easily distracted by what we see (cherry pie a la mode or mashed potatoes and gravy). and all our good intentions go down the throat.

So, facing up to the fact that I was one who needed rewards, I continued to work on my structure until I could see it actually shedding its antiquated rooms and. becoming the slim, sleek bungalow of my blueprint—a fitting temple for the Lord.

9

Planing the Boards

As the numbers decreased on the scale and previously undiscovered bones made their appearance, I noticed something else. In place of the bulges were little folds of skin. I had flaps on my elbows!

Although good skin tone had been retained through slow weight loss, there was some looseness, and my spirit as well as my muscles drooped.

And I wasn't the only one who noticed. One day while dusting, I heard my little girl snicker. Glancing over my shoulder, I saw her watching my every move. But, in a hurry to finish my housework, I continued dusting the lampshades and picture frames until finally her peals of laughter stopped me.

"What's so funny?" I asked, looking around the room. "Is the cat chasing her tail again?"

"No," she giggled.

"Oh, are you listening to the radio with your earplug?" I said, lifting her long, blonde hair.

"No," she tittered.

"Well, what? Tell me; I want to laugh, too."

"Oh, Mom, it looks so funny when you dust. The skin on the back of your arms jiggles and quivers like Jello."

It didn't make me laugh. I knew I would have to do something to firm up my muscles—not just on my arms, but also on the front and back porch of my building project. But what?

That unsavory word, *exercise,* leaped into my mind, with all its boring antics and painful gyrations. I simply didn't want to spend half an hour a day kicking, jumping and stretching. There must be a better way to firm up. A fun way.

My friend, Rusty, keeps fit by swimming, but unfortunately, I'm not a swimmer. Not that I haven't tried. I've taken swimming lessons three times as an adult. I sink when I tread water, choke when I breathe, and splash in everyone's eyes with my thrashing. My children refuse to go swimming with me if any of their friends are near by.

Lois roller-skates. I tried that a few years ago, too, and ended up in the hospital with a ruptured disk.

I even took a stab at fencing—our backyard, with six-foot grapestakes. But that couldn't be classified as exercise (or a fence either, for that matter).

Enough negatives. I have found several forms of exercise I enjoy, and feel sure that after some consideration, you'll find a type of exercise you like, too.

How about bike riding? It takes very little skill, only the ability to balance and an appreciation of the outdoors. Where I live, I can bike most of the year. However, those living in snow country would have to do something else during the winter months— shoveling?

When I started biking, I thought it would be a good family exercise. But my husband, an avid athlete, rode so fast he left me in the backdraft. So, I found it better to ride alone or with another lady friend.

And I didn't coast along. For biking to do my heart and muscles much good, I learned that I had to ride hard enough to produce a light perspiration on my forehead. Anything less strenuous was fun but not fruitful.

Or, how about tennis? I finally took lessons at the encouragement of my family and, as a beginner, I still spend most of my time chasing the ball in other players' courts. Here is a game that uses muscles in every part of the body, and I think that with practice and a partner that plays as poorly as I, I could really become addicted to this sport. Even without a partner, hitting the ball against the backboard is good exercise. And my family has patiently played with me until I can almost return the ball to my ten-year-old.

But what about those days when I don't want to get outside? Remember the jump rope? I have one of those with handles that are stationary as the rope goes around and around and—whoops—around. I started by setting my timer for one minute, then added a minute each day until I was jumping five or more minutes at a time. I think it's my favorite form for firming.

Perhaps none of this appeals to you. In fact, every form of exercise reminds you of a day in the Colosseum with the lions. Have you tried walking? Almost everyone walks—to the refrigerator for a glass of milk, to the TV to transform the Three Stooges into Robert Redford, and to the mailbox for bills and bulletins.

I've tried walking a little faster and farther. I don't park next to the door when I shop anymore, but at the far end of the parking lot. And walking to the neighborhood store not only saves gas, but maybe my life.

There may be some reading this who are incapacitated and unable to walk or exercise, and firming up your body through physical effort is impossible. But you, as well as I, can exercise the mind and spirit in several ways. By reading—good books, newspapers, and the Bible. We can also pray—for others, for ourselves, and for God's glory. And it's easy to smile—an exercise that beautifies any face.

Smiling can make an intolerable circumstance seem less forboding. It lifts the spirits of both the giver and the receiver. Really, a smile is the best exercise of all!

So, to keep the temple in shape after reaching my weight goal, I continued to plane the boards through exercise and maintenance of my new eating habits. I knew now was not the time to return to my old habits, or one day I would wake up to find the same fat body I had had before.

I admit that continually watching what I eat is distasteful. I would rather forget about dieting for the rest of my life. But I can't, anymore than, as a Christian, I can return to my old sinful way of life.

To grow as a child of God, there must be discipline. I know I should read the Bible daily and obey the commands and precepts I find there if I want to mature and enjoy fellowship with God. And as a fit temple for the Lord, I must keep my body and appetites under control by following a sensible diet and exercise plan.

"But I keep under my body, and bring it into subjection . . ." (I Corinthians 9:27a). Is it easy? Is anything worthwhile easy? I've been married over twenty-five years now, and although I have always respected and loved my husband, it hasn't always been easy to live with him. Our personalities clash in many ways. He storms while I bite my tongue. I cry while he remains cool. When I want to go out to dinner, he wants to stay home and read. And when he wants to go bike riding, I want to stay home and read.

But we both want God's will. And so we work at our marriage. We take turns giving in. (We also take turns not giving in.) It isn't always easy, but we are building a relationship that is strong and durable, and as winds and storms come against our temples from time to time, we hold fast to each other and to our God—and stand.

Likewise, honoring and glorifying God in my body isn't always easy, but I can "be strong in the Lord, and in the power of his might" (Ephesians 6:10).

In looking over my list of changes, I can't really cross off item number one, because I must continue to diet and exercise. But I will put a little star next to it to symbolize my success in slimming down my building. You know, the years after forty seem brighter every day, and I eagerly move on to the next improvement on my blueprint for the back forty.

10

Shingling the Roof

How thrilled I was to have finally lost those twenty pounds, for I not only looked younger and healthier, I felt it.

After successfully completing the first item on my blueprint for the back forty, I quickly moved on to shingle my roof with the next two projects on my list—*HAIR* and *FACE*. I could take care of both problems at the same time, thereby checking off numbers two and three on my blueprint.

Neither change was phenomenal, yet I could see an immediate improvement and felt my self-esteem beginning to grow. And, believe me, those of us passing through the middle-age mopes need all the confidence we can get.

Since each of us applies makeup and arranges hair to suit ourselves, I'll only comment briefly on what I did. (Who knows? I may change again next week.)

I used a natural color rinse to blend in the gray hairs that were sprouting as quickly as a new lawn on a spring day. They still show through, but now have a bright shine that gives the illusion of freshly frosted hair—something I paid for with pain and purse for many years. And, cut in a style that doesn't need hair spray (that makes my husband happy), my hair is easier to care for. Check off Number 2.

On to Number 3. After trying several moisturizers, I found one that suited not only my skin, but also my budget, and was amazed how my dry skin sucked up the moisture. I also began consistently using cream for those smile wrinkles around my eyes and mouth. Of course, I have to face the inevitability of the aging process, but I feel that I'm easing into it more gracefully now.

While searching for God's plan in shingling my roof, I found something even better than creams and blushers to erase wrinkles and give the face a glow— something to crown my building with more strength and beauty than the finest roof in town.

At this point in my building project, discouragement began to set in. My life hadn't suddenly become as full and thrilling as I had imagined it would. In fact, changes began to take place in my home that hurt and disappointed me beyond words.

My oldest son had left home and was living with some rock musicians who had little, if any, regard for God or their families. He joined them in their philosophy and way of life, and began to sink deeper and deeper into their counterculture.

Shortly afterward, one of my daughters began dating a young man who had a detrimental influence on her, driving a wedge of bitterness between mother and daughter.

I wondered if I would ever see these two reconciled to us and to God; and if not, what hope could I hold for my other children who were looking up to them? So I worried. I prayed. I admonished. I cried. And finally I learned a beautiful lesson—one that turned my children around, and became the covering on my temple for the Lord.

I shingled my roof with *praise*. Praise to the God who deserves not only honor and glory, but also my trust. Why had it taken me so long to learn such a basic Christian principle? Paul exhorts in Philippians 4:4, "Rejoice in the Lord alway: and again I say, Rejoice."

And in I Thessalonians 5:18, we are encouraged— no, commanded—to give thanks for everything. Thanks for *everything?* How could I thank God for children who were alienated and distant from Him? And besides, they were hurting *me*. I couldn't thank God for that. Or could I?

I had read many books written by victorious Christians instructing their readers on the value of praise. They told how their lives had been transformed as they began to exercise the attitude of gratitude. But this was different. This was *MY* problem. Those others were only words in books.

But, after trying everything else with frustration and anxiety as the end result, where else could I turn? I was up against, not a wall this time, but a roof. I had to find something to cover my vulnerability to the freezing cold of disappointment and the hot rays of embarrassment. I *had* to begin praising God.

At first, they were only words. I didn't *FEEL* thankful for the circumstances as they were. I wanted to interject directions to God as to how He should work things out. *How could this be happening to me?* I questioned. *Me, a Christian mother whose greatest desire is that my children love and honor You.*

But, little by little, as I praised without feeling it became easier, and soon my feelings caught up with my act of faith. I was praising God and meaning it!

He *did* know what was best. He *did* have a perfect plan. And although I didn't see His complete answer for my son until three years after I began pleading, it was only a few months after I began praising God that my son committed his life to Jesus Christ and married a Christian girl. Today he has just completed his college education with honors.

Praise God!

The answer, through praise, came even quicker for my daughter. After I had spent many months begging God to show her the reality of His Son, just one night of praising Him for her just as she was brought her to her knees, seeking His cleansing and filling. And the change in her life has been remarkable. Christ is in control. "Whoso offereth praise glorifieth me . . ." (Psalms 50:23a).

I've shared both of these experiences because they were not only a turning point in my own life-after-forty, but also a climax in the lives of my children. Praise to God is the only suitable covering for a temple of the Lord. As each shingle is comprised of a word of thanksgiving, then fitted together side by side, they cover the roof with one glorious paean of praise.

The roof points to Heaven in acknowledgment of Him who sits on the throne ordering lives and nations according to His will, for it is a sovereign God we praise. Nothing surprises Him. Nothing upsets Him. All things are working together for good to them who love Him and are called according to His purpose (Romans 8:28).

So, in believing that all things work together for our good, we can face reality. There will be problems on the back forty, perhaps greater ones than we encountered on the south forty. Changes come quickly now. Children leave home. Husbands retire. Loved ones pass away. There could be a move to a convalescent home or hospital one day where a long-lingering illness may sap away our strength. Who knows what lies ahead?

God knows. And because He knows and cares, there is no need to fear the back forty years. With a temple built on the right foundation—faith in Jesus Christ—and covered with an enduring roof—praise for Him who knows and does all things well—we can face anything that comes into our lives with confidence, not in our meager resources, but in God, the Almighty One.

Praise the Lord!

11

Painting the House

California is unique in its menu of tasteful decorating ideas, and in some neighborhoods you can find colors ranging from enriched white to wheat brown, with all the mustard yellows and catsup reds sandwiched between.

The occupants unknowingly reveal something of themselves through their color schemes—some have no taste at all, while others are absolutely gourmet in their choices.

My husband, a gulping gourmet, chose a delicate beige tone for the front of our house. But more pressing activities (hiking, biking, tennis) intruded on his house-painting plans, so there on the garage shelf with other unused cans, sat the paint. Until one day . . .

"Mom, why are you setting up the ladder and wearing those gross clothes?" my teenager asked.

"I'm going to surprise Dad," I said, prying off the lid and watching the paint "glug" into the tray. "He'll be so pleased—and so will the neighbors."

With an early start and no lunch break, I had finished before my husband walked in the door for dinner.

I wanted to surprise you by painting the front of the house. Are you surprised?

"What have you done?" he asked, a mixture of unbelief and fear punctuating his words.

"Well, I wanted to surprise you by painting the front of the house. Are you surprised?"

"Am I!" he wheezed. "You used the right paint, didn't you?"

"Sure, the pale beige. Good thing I finished on time, too. It looks like rain."

Peering out the window next morning, my stomach flip-flopped. "Honey, come here and look. I think some kind of fungus attacked our shrubbery overnight!"

I wanted to cry as he pointed out my error in using the paint bought for the family room—paint which had run off onto the shrubs and flowers. All my plans to make a good impression were washed up.

How about the paint job on my building project? I didn't want a covering that would wash off on a rainy day. I had lost weight, changed my hairstyle and softened my wrinkles, but what did my back forty exterior really convey of who lived inside?

I hoped others saw me as a self-giving, spiritual Christian; but I knew I often came across as a self-centered egotist. How could I know who and what I truly am and really show it? And how could I be genuinely interested in others and honor the Lord in my body and spirit, if, in my heart, I was always thinking about myself?

Many questions. Again, I found the answers in the Bible. "For as he thinketh in his heart, so is he . . ." (Proverbs 23:7a). In other words, what I *think* is what I *am*. If I act like a self-centered person, it's because I am thinking self-centered thoughts. If I want to be a loving person, I must think loving thoughts—thoughts that will change my actions and, more particularly, my reactions.

Simplistic as it sounds, my thought life seemed to fall into three categories: what I think of myself, what I think of others, and what I think of God. So, although I'm not a psychologist, I'll just pass along my discoveries as one friend to another.

1. *What do I think of myself?* I often sway from one side to the other with either an inflated or deflated opinion of myself. I admit I frequently react like Susan when unpleasant discussions arise. She is the good-natured, always smiling deaconess—until someone disagrees with her.

Then her icy-cold stare could bring chills on a hot summer day (might be good to have her inflated ego around if the air-conditioning fails).

Do I also get on a high horse when my plans are thwarted? I'm afraid so. Oh, I don't usually give the cold shoulder, but I swallow my anger with a smile while inwardly I bubble and boil until I spew over on my family or some other unsuspecting person. Unfortunately, many hurt feelings have come about in Christian circles through such unsurrendered superiority complexes.

Sometimes I laugh and ridicule those who claim, in loud boisterous voices, "I am the greatest," but I'm just as foolish because eventually my thoughts of grandeur will show through. Then others, seeing my pride and hostility, will know that I, too, am a proud, arrogant person. And all the while I thought I was hiding it. As a man thinketh in his heart, *so, is he* (and so is *she*).

Then there's the opposite—the person who is always down. His thoughts are wrong, too. "I can't do anything right. Everyone is more talented than I. No one understands me."

No one can get close to an inferiority complex, either, because self-centered thoughts wall us off from fellowship with each other. I've experienced my share of despondency, too, and those passing through the middle-age mopes may find depressing thoughts flitting through or even controlling the mind at times. But, if such thoughts are allowed to continue, serious personality changes may occur.

How can these wrong thoughts be conquered? "For I say," writes Paul, "through the grace given unto me, to every man that is among you, not to think of himself more highly [nor lowly] than he ought to think . . ." (Romans 12:3a).

Can I really help what I think? I have thought patterns that have developed over the years. When others built me up or put me down, I believed them. Their opinions, right or wrong, influenced my thinking.

Good news. There is One stronger than all who have gone before. " . . . greater is he that is in you, than he that is in the world" (I John 4:4b). God can change my mind about myself by giving me a glimpse of His thoughts toward me as revealed in the Bible.

In John 15:15, He calls me His friend: "Henceforth I call you not servants; for the servant knoweth not what his lord doeth: but I have called you friends; for all things that I have heard of my Father I have made known unto you." I'm His friend!

He goes even further in Ephesians 5:30, for in this passage Paul says, "We are members of his [Christ's] body, of his flesh, and of his bones." I'm part of His body!

John 17:23 is the ultimate of Christ's thinking toward me: "I in them, and thou in me, that they may be made perfect in one; and that the world may know that thou has sent me, and hast loved them, as thou hast loved me." He loves me! Read Psalm 139 to be truly convinced.

If these words are true (and they are, because they are God's own words), then I must believe them, and every time I am tempted to lift myself up or put myself down, I can recall His words, repeating them audibly. And before long, my thoughts about myself will be God's thoughts.

2. *What do I think of others?* Should I be honest? Sometimes they drive me up a wall. People can be so insensitive, inefficient, and lacking in character. And, while I think I'm hiding my thoughts with a friendly smile, they know what I'm really thinking. And if they already happen to have a low self-image, an inferiority complex may develop, stunting their growth. Or, if they are on the same ego trip as I, our personalities will surely clash.

Why do I harbor such critical attitudes of others? I've found I'm most critical when others aren't conforming to my ideas of how they should treat *ME*. They aren't giving me the attention, respect and care that I want. Ugly, isn't it? Are you ever critical of those who don't act out the scripts you've written for them?

Husband: Gives me everything I want. Appreciates all I do for him and shows it. Gives me his undivided attention when I want it, and leaves me alone when I don't.

Children: Obey instantly. Respect my every wish. Choose nice friends. Made good grades.

Friends: Find me their most interesting companion. Always available when I need them. Agree with my ideas and philosophies.

Spiritual leaders: Counsel me with understanding

and love. Give top-notch messages (that fit my preconceived ideas). Without fault.

Everyone else: Fits into my plans.

The problem is that each person in my life has a script, too, but written with a different *STAR*. I want to be the star, and so does he or she. So how can I resolve my playacting and begin, in God's will, to relate to others?

I must first recognize that God has written the script for my final act, the back forty; then I need only learn the lines and watch the plot thicken.

"Let nothing be done through strife or vainglory; but in lowliness of mind let each esteem other better than themselves" (Philippians 2:3). And, get this . . .

"A new commandment I give unto you, That ye love one another; as I have loved you, that ye also love one another" (John 13:34).

So when I am tempted to belittle others in my mind, instead I should deliberately think God's thoughts and begin to love them. And they'll know it because I'll show it.

3. And then, most important, *what do I think of God?* Do I imagine Him as a benevolent Spirit somewhere way out there who bends down to help me when I call? Or do I see Him as an angry Judge who will slap me when I sin?

There are possibly as many ideas of God as there are persons. Each one—yes, even those who claim the name of Christ—has his own interpretation of God. And perhaps our powerlessness and ineffectiveness is the result of our creating a powerless and ineffective God in our minds.

But once again, the Bible comes to our rescue. "The Lord is righteous in all his ways, and holy in all His works" (Psalm 145:17). He is Righteousness.

"For if our heart condemn us, God is greater than our heart, and knoweth all things" (I John 3:20). He is Knowledge.

"Ah Lord God! behold, thou has made the heaven and the earth by thy great power and stretched out arm, and there is nothing too hard for thee" (Jeremiah 32:17). He is Power.

"And God said unto Moses. *I AM THAT I AM:* and he said, Thus shalt thou say unto the children of Israel, *I AM* hath sent me unto you" (Exodus 3:14). He Is—everything I could ever want or need.

So, whenever I am tempted to fit God into my own little mold, I can search the Scriptures and there find the only true God and Jesus Christ whom God sent.

And with my thinking right about myself, others and God, my outward appearance begins to take on a glow, one that reflects the Occupant, rather than the occupant.

For I must remember, this building project is not for *self,* but is a temple for the Lord. His occupancy in my life will hopefully attract others to develop the parcel of land they have left, for God deserves the best—whatever our age.

Yes, I have found a paint that will endure—and a thought life that if practiced, will glorify God and bless those I encounter on my newly developed frontier—the back forty.

12

Living in the Room

Boy, oh, boy, did I have some plans for the day! First, straighten the house, then get to my typewriter for the rest of the day. I had lots of good ideas for an article, and planned to spend the entire day writing. A day to myself. Oh, glory!

"Brrrringggg!" Now, who could that be? Well, I'd get rid of whoever it was in a hurry—somehow.

"Oh, hi, Julie. How've you been? Not so good, huh? You want to come over? Today? Well, I don't know. Just a minute, let me see."

I set down the receiver and rattled the pages of my appointment book. "Oh, Julie, I'm so sorry. It looks like I have a doctor's appointment. Maybe another time, okay?"

I hung up the phone. I felt awful—guilty. Kind of nauseous and breathless. She had sounded worried and stopped up like she'd been crying. Oh, well, I'd call her later. She'd probably have her problem solved by then, and I'd have my article written.

Sitting at the typewriter, all those good ideas vanished into the ceiling. I couldn't think about anything but Julie. She needed to talk, and had chosen me to share her problem. And I had dismissed her as easily as a patient in an overcrowded hospital.

I picked up the phone. "Julie," I said in a too-high voice, "listen, I just realized that my appointment is for later in the week (it really was), so come on over."

As I hung up, the tight band I'd felt around my chest loosened and fell off. Once more I was available. God had a plan for my day that didn't include my typewriter. And He'd help me get those ideas on paper at a later time. I knew He would.

Julie had a problem all right, a serious one. But after sharing some promises from the Bible and praying together, she left feeling less desperate and more confident that "all things work together for good to them that love God . . ." (Romans 8:28).

That day I began to see what my back forty living room could be like.

In our home, we do most of our living in the family room and keep the living room neat and uncluttered. It's great to have one room where we can welcome guests without blushing. It's an attractive room, furnished with marble-topped tables, stereo, brass planters, and a lovely curio cabinet. But something's missing. It doesn't have life.

Although that may be fine for my *actual* home (my husband thinks it's marvelous to have one room where he can sit without school books, stamp collections and banana peels decorating the tables), I felt that I had taken the same untouchable attitude with my life's living room, God's temple. I had wanted to keep a room just for myself, one that was always neat and uncluttered. But, in closing myself off, I had lost the awareness of others. My back forty living room had to be different. I would learn to

LIVE, to be aware.

Most of the time, I was preoccupied with either the past or the future: "I wish I'd said . . ." or, "Someday I'd like to . . .," and I was seldom aware of the *NOW.* Perhaps that was why the presence of God eluded me.

He is the God of the present. *He is.*

Oh, there's that phone again. Who can it be this time? "Hello. Oh, Betty, how are you? You're on your way over? Sure, come on. I'd like to hear about the Bible study you went to last night." Ah, that's better.

I once read that a person totally yielded to the Lord will have a path beaten to his door as thirsty souls reach out for the water of life. I've never been oversupplied with friends, probably because I've been unavailable, but I can see that, as I'm committed to Jesus Christ, He will draw others to me. And it excites me to consider the possibilities of my back forty living room.

Living is *now.* God is *now.* And to be aware, fully aware of Him and life, I must be still and know that He is God—*now* (Psalm 46:10a). I think the secret to living in the present and learning to accept the interruptions and irritations that come into my day is simply to believe that God is in everything. That phone call. That broken appointment. That postponed wedding. God is in it. He is life. He is now.

In the past, I've found it easier to think about tomorrow than to face up to today. Today's problems hurt. Today's people annoy. Today's challenges frighten. But if God is in everything. *If* . . .

When I am still, still from my own plans, prejudices and preconceived ideas, I am aware of God around me, and life takes on new depth. The birds' songs are cheerier. The cat's coat furrier. The children's smiles merrier. Even the irritations and heartaches become bearable, perhaps a little lovely, when I acknowledge God in them.

Is it scriptural to believe that God is in everything—that there are no second causes in the life of the Christian? The Bible says that not even a sparrow falls to the ground without God's knowledge. The hairs of my head are numbered (Matthew 10:29,30). He knows the way that I take. Nothing can separate me from the love of God. There are so many promises that assure me of God's love and presence that I can rest in His daily plan for my life—and live.

I really want to be aware—aware of God's working in my life, aware of the needs of those around me, aware of Him and His creation.

On my back forty, I've only just begun—to live.

13

Turning on the Stove

"Honey," my husband said after four months of what I thought was wedded bliss, "I don't want to hurt you, but I can't stand tuna casserole."

What a shock! I'd been serving it twice a week with never an indication that he didn't enjoy it. Hurt and certain our marriage was over, I ran from the room with him following close behind. Then, gently taking me in his arms, he assured me that, "Even if I don't like tuna casserole, I do love you."

Although I haven't served that particular dish for the past twenty-five years, I've gotten into similar ruts in my menu variations. There were the hamburger days when I tried every dish in my *250 Recipes for Ground Meat;* the potato craze in which I prepared spuds from scalloped to pancaked; and the cheese phase when we ate Swiss and Cheddar in and on everything from salad to pie.

I learned that those bad habits were what added unwanted pounds, and now that I had lost those pounds, I planned to change my menus to ones of greater nutrition and variety.

The kitchen in my back forty home would be more fruitful (and vegetableful) than my south forty kitchen.

Even though my grocery budget was larger now than in those first tuna years, much of it was wasted on junk foods. Convinced by TV hawkers that children needed potato chips and presweetened cereals to become well-adjusted adults, I had regularly added those items to my grocery list. No more. There may yet be time to instill good eating habits in the three left at home.

But how they squawked at first! "Mom, there's nothing to eat" (only fruit for snacks).

"What's this stuff?" (broccoli, steamed to a lush green).

"Where's the cereal?" (three boxes of high protein and bran cereals staring down from the shelf).

My husband was delighted because he has always preferred fresh fruit and vegetables to sweets and starch. (No wonder he has never had a weight problem.)

Eating nutritious food doesn't need to be boring, either. I have a variety of cookbooks with countless ways of preparing deliciously attractive meals. And it's fun trying new things.

One week we visited the Riviera through *"Adventures in French Cooking.* Another time, we were part of the jet-set as I experimented with *Great Dishes of the World.* I even have a lovely cookbook put out by the American Heart Association with recipes low in cholesterol and unsaturated fats.

Since I want to keep my husband alive longer, I plan to watch his diet. I wonder how many of us bury our husbands prematurely with poorly planned menus high in fats and cholesterol. Especially if a husband is overweight, he should be helped—not by nagging, for no man wants another mother telling

We were part of the jet set as I experimented
with "Great Dishes of the World."

him how to eat. But his eating habits can be changed by preparing the right foods in a tasty manner, without his ever knowing what's happening. Eventually, he'll be so satisfied, he'll even lose his taste for high calorie dishes.

Yes, even though today's women, with convenience foods, don't have to spend as much time in the kitchen, its still an important room. The working woman doesn't have much time, but she, too, can plan at least one meal a day where the members of the family can gather around the table. Granted, as the children grow older, their activities—school functions, jobs and friends—demand more of their time, but it's well worth the effort to fit in an occasional meal together.

I try to remember that dinner is not the time to tell my son that he needs a haircut, or my daughter to quit punctuating her sentences with, "you know." I say, *Keep the conversation pleasant. It helps the digestion—you know.*

But there's more to supplying our daily needs than the preparation of good food. Jesus said, "'Man shall not live by bread alone, but by every word of God" (Luke 4:4).

Conversations about God and His place in our lives arise easily and naturally in the warm atmosphere of the kitchen. I think standing over the stove stirring hot soup is a better setting than a pulpit to listen to my daughter's problems and counsel her from God's Word. And I find many opportunities to worship God in my kitchen, too.

Often my days are so busy and hectic, there simply isn't time to bow the knees and seek His face, but God is always available and always present. He enjoys my worship as much when I am rolling out a pie crust as He does in the church pew.

I'm not saying there isn't a need for the quiet time; *I* need it. But when there are problems or praises to be offered, He hears, wherever I am. A good example of worshipping God in the kitchen is the old classic, "Practicing the Presence of God," by Brother Lawrence.

I've found one of my least favorite chores, ironing, is a great time to intercede for the members of my family. Gliding the iron over my husband's shirts (no big deal with all the permanent-press fabrics), I lift him up before the throne of God. *Thank You for this man of mine. Bless and give him strength to labor for his family. Bring special surprises that give him unexpected joy in his life today. And help me to show him how much I love him.*

Then smoothing out a beautifully embroidered workshirt, I pray, *Keep my daughter in the center of Your will today. Help her to see that John is not right for her. His disinterest in spiritual things is drawing her away from Your fellowship.*

And, *Give my son wisdom as he pursues his education,* I pray, avoiding the pearl snaps on a Western shirt. *Help him to see that, although the testing now is grievous, afterward it will yield a peaceable fruit.*

I find myself praying for the friends of each one, too; and even reaching out to mission fields and those whom I've never seen.

Scrubbing the floor doesn't have to be a lesson in drudgery, either. Watching the dirt rinse out of a soapy mop as a bright shiny floor emerges can be just the time to examine my life for unconfessed sin. And, as the words spill out in agreement with God, I experience the cleansing effect in my life that I see taking place on the kitchen floor.

Yes, there are many object lessons to be learned through kitchen duties, but the primary purpose of consuming food points to the importance of spiritual food for Christian growth.

The Word of God is likened to water, milk, bread, meat and honey because, as food is necessary to physical growth, so is the Bible necessary to spiritual growth. Neglected even one day, there is a loss of strength. And if several days or weeks go by without feeding on God's Word, loss of appetite occurs. Where there is a loss of appetite, there will be sickness, weakness and perhaps an early death.

I've experienced a deadness of spirit and can always trace it back to a lack of partaking of the Word of God. Sometimes I even have to force-feed myself when there is no hunger for God's Word; but, once begun and pursued, a healthy appetite returns.

It's not enough just to read a passage through a sense of duty. For the Bible to benefit us spiritually, the Holy Spirit must be allowed to teach. "But the Comforter, which is the Holy Ghost, whom the Father will send in my name, he shall teach you all things, and bring all things to your remembrance, whatsoever I have said unto you" (John 14:26).

I like to study with several different questions in mind (and on paper).

1. What can I learn about God through this passage?
2. What promise can I claim?
3. What sin should I forsake?
4. What work can I do?

Seeking God's will with an open mind and heart feeds my spirit, as well as gives me food to share with others.

So, as I prepare better meals in my back forty kitchen, I also prepare myself through God's Word to be a better person in my back forty years. And as I do, I am confident that my building, bought with a price, is growing into a temple that will glorify God.

14

Putting up the Antenna

"Mom . . ."

"Just a minute, honey. I want to hear what this guy's saying."

"But, Mom . . ."

"Shhh, can't you see I'm watching TV?"

"But . . ."

"Oh, what is it? Honestly, you can be so thoughtless!"

"I just wanted to thank you for ironing my blouse— and, well, I love you."

With those words, my daughter, eyes misting, shuffled out of the family room.

Family room? Hardly. Although we didn't fight and roar at each other (that would classify it as a den), neither did we really share as a family. That particular room in our home had become a boob-icle tube-icle cubicle, a launching pad into the world of make-believe. And I couldn't shift the blame to my husband (he prefers reading in the living room), or my children (they love to talk and play games). *I* was to blame.

Oh, I was fairly selective about what I watched— no excessive violence or offensive sex. But too much

The family room had become a launching pad
into the world of make-believe.

time passed with glazed eyes focused on the box in the corner, instead of seeking out ways to develop our home life. I was able to rationalize my time before the television by reading during the commercials, but couldn't justify the garbage my children were assimilating.

It was just easier to turn on the tube than read my youngest a bedtime story; and discussing chemistry certainly didn't measure up to "Blood and Thunder in the Suburbs." I had been "copping out."

Not only was I wasting time and ignoring my family, I began to realize that coarse dialogue and ungodly subjects which would never have been permitted on TV five or ten years ago were pouring into my home. And I wasn't getting anything out of my reading, either. It was hard to concentrate on a book expounding the holiness of God while two men in the corner plotted the murder of their wives.

The family room in my back forty home needed remodeling, and it would begin with the television. I'm sure Jesus didn't have TV in mind when He said, "Blessed are those servants, whom the lord when he cometh shall find watching . . ." (Luke 12:37).

The problem isn't just the television, and I'm not going to throw ours out or take down the antenna; it's the lack of having my own antenna up— watching and listening for the cries and laughter of my family. And, more particularly, listening for the quiet, barely perceptible Word from God.

Maybe Paul had today's Christians in mind when he wrote, using the initials TV to make his point, ". . . sirs, why do ye these things? We also are men of like passions with you, and preach unto you that ye should *T*urn from these *V*anities unto the living God, which made heaven, and earth, and the sea, and all things that are therein" (Acts 14:15).

I'm just playing with our English words; Paul wrote in Greek, but it's true: much of what is offered on TV today could be called "vanity." Read God's definition of the word in the Book of Ecclesiastes.

However, I don't think it's enough for me to turn *from* something—that only feeds my ego and gives me a legalistic attitude. I must turn *to* the living God and consider Him. And by putting Him first in my times of relaxation, I find my antenna up and ready to receive all kinds of messages, not only from God, but also from my family.

What fun I'm now having in my back forty family room! We've learned to needlepoint. We've made some beautiful Doodle-Art pictures, and are now reading aloud from Grimm's Fairy Tales. Even my teenagers (though they don't like to admit it) enjoy these way-out, sometimes gory stories. And talking together over puzzles and games has opened up opportunities to heal some old wounds that had been hurting.

But, above all, we have more time now to consider God's plan for our lives through reading the Bible, good Christian books, and just talking things over.

We're not perfect or pious and, more often than I care to confess, we slip back into old habits. But we're learning and growing, and one day when my children have all left home, I'll have warm memories of laughter and fun in the family room—not just cold images of make-believe families who solved their problems in thirty minutes—without God.

"Mom . . ."

"Just a minute, honey. Let me finish writing this paragraph. Okay, shoot."

"Will you help me with the introduction to my essay?"

"Sure, if you'll help me finish off this chapter of my book."

"Well," she said after reading a few minutes, "how about, 'Now in my back forty family room we're all on the same channel and coming in loud and clear'?"

"Great! Say, you're so good—write your own introduction."

15

Lighting the Fire

"1-2-3-4-5," I whispered across the table, my chin resting lightly on my fingertips.

"Huh?"

Stretching my lips into a wide smile, I asked, "6-7-8-9-10?"

"What are you doing?"

"Oh, 11-12," I added, corrugating my brow.

My husband glanced over his shoulder to see if the waiter was nearby, then leaned toward me, almost upsetting his glass of water. "Why are you counting—like that?"

I did feel a little silly, but at least it worked. I had his attention.

"Well," I hemmed, "we've practically finished our dinner in silence and, I don't know, it looks like we're bored with each other. And I just thought we could at least *look* like we're having a good time."

"I'm having a good time," my husband said, chomping his medium-well New York steak. "Aren't you? What's the matter, your meat tough?"

"No."

"No, what?"

"No, my steak's not tough, and no, I'm not having

82

a good time."

"Oh," he said, ending the conversation.

I looked around the restaurant. There were young couples animatedly talking and holding hands across the table. Some tables were filled with friends or families laughing and conversing.

If Bill and Janet had come with us, my husband would be talking, too, about either his work, his hobbies or years gone by. Why didn't he talk to *me?* Was I so boring? I decided to try again.

"Oh, guess what?" I bubbled. "The doorbell rang today, and I was so surprised to see the mailman standing there. As you know, he always just leaves the mail in the box. So I wondered what on earth he could want."

"Oh, yeah—what was the problem?" he asked, his fork poised in the air.

"Well, it seems there was two cents postage due— on an advertisement! Can you believe it? Ha, ha."

"Really? Hmmm."

Once again the silence stretched between us. I stirred the events of the day in my mind, hoping for another tidbit to serve him. I'd already dished out the skinned knee, the broken flowerpot and the cat climbing the drapes. Oh, well, I'd just be quiet and concentrate on my dinner, too.

Over twenty-five years of marriage and we didn't have anything to talk about. Come to think of it, he had always been the strong, silent type. In fact, that was one of the things I'd liked about him. He wasn't flippant. When he said something, it was worth listening to.

He never discussed people or personalities, either. Not even under the guise of a prayer request— another thing I'd admired. Why did the very things that attracted me then irritate me now? It hadn't bothered me until recently, probably because I had been so preoccupied with children most of our married life. But the time was rapidly approaching when there would be just the two of us.

Good grief, three times a day we'd be sitting across the table from each other staring at our plates. Something must be done. I would try to become more interesting and better informed, and thus, a more desirable dinner companion.

So, for the next few weeks I boned up on tax shelters and income properties, but still our conversations bombed. It seemed he didn't want to discuss business over chicken a la king. Then I tried reading books about famous war battles and generals. But the book reports with bacon and eggs only sent him off to work ready to fight.

A different strategy was in order. I dressed up in the evenings in fancy dresses and musk perfume, but he still didn't change. Okay, if it's silence he wants, it's silence he'll get. I didn't talk. I didn't even smile. I was ugly. But if he noticed, he didn't say anything. He just smiled sweetly, kissed and thanked me for such a delicious meal.

Oh, he made me so mad. How could a guy be thoughtful, loving, appreciative and, yes, even romantic, and not "communicate"? All the articles and books on marriage stress the importance of communication. And to me, that meant *TALK*. Why wouldn't he change?

It was really beginning to bug me. I was sure other men talked problems over with their wives. Joan's husband tells her all the things that worry him at the office. Then he spends the evening sleeping on the couch while she worries about possible bankruptcy.

Tara and Steve talk. Loud—and in front of everyone. But, at least they're communicating, and the experts say that's good. Personally, I wish they'd do their communicating in the privacy of their own home.

My frustration began to build. What would it be like in ten or twenty years? How could he be so happy, and I so, not unhappy, but discontented? I wanted him to change. I wanted him to talk. I wanted him to notice me. I wanted . . .

I wanted God's will. What was it, anyway? Did He have anything to say about my problem? Back to the Rule Book—Ephesians, chapter five.

First, I read that I should understand the will of the Lord, then thank Him for all things (verses 17,20).

Next, it said I had to submit myself to my husband as I would to the Lord, recognizing my relationship with him symbolizes the relationship between the church and Christ (verses 22-24).

And last of all, in verse 33, I found that I was to reverence, or honor and respect, my husband.

There are also many verses scattered throughout the chapter instructing the husband in his responsibility to the wife; but, as that wasn't my concern, I focused on my obedience to the Lord, and left the results to Him.

I went over it again. What did it mean to understand the will of the Lord? I find His will revealed throughout the Bible, and although I may rationalize and rebel, I must believe that His way is the best way—the only way I will be truly happy.

Then, by faith, I must thank Him always for all things in the name of Jesus Christ. Thank Him *sometimes* for *some things?* No. *Always* for *all things:* not in my own name or nature, but in Jesus !

"Wives, submit yourselves unto your own husbands, as unto the Lord" (Ephesians 5:22). Ouch! That verse would bring fire to the eyes of any red-blooded women's libber. And it used to bother me, too. I was submissive outwardly; but a true submission as to the Lord would mean I submit because I want to—because I love.

These verses seem to be saying that, even if I don't always agree with or understand my husband's ways, I will subject myself willingly to him in everything because he is my head. This passage sets out God's perfect plan for a Christian marriage: Christ over the husband; the husband over the wife; and the parents over the children. Any other form of family government leads to anarchy.

Then I looked at verse 33 again. ". . . and the wife see that she reverence her husband."

Some women choke and turn blue. "You gotta be kiddin'," they say. "Reverence that fat slob?"

Maybe if he were shown more respect and honor, he wouldn't be a fat slob. Most of us try to live up to others' opinions of us. "Make him your king," the Lord is saying. Lay your gifts of love at his feet. He may kick you in the face at first because he didn't expect you to be there but after awhile he'll begin to behave royally and love you as he loves himself.

I closed my Bible. I could see God's solution to my problem, but it took awhile before I was willing to admit it. I was wrong. I had been trying to change my husband—and he knew it. If there were any changes to be made, I would have to be the one to make them.

And wasn't that what I really wanted for my back forty? Change? I rephrased Philippians 4:11 to read, ". . . with whatsoever mate I have, therewith to be content." That would be a change.

I loved my husband. I even admired and respected him. But I hadn't really been content and accepted him for who and what he is. I decided to make a list (again), this time writing down all his good points and his not-so-good points, just to see him more objectively. Then I compared them. The good far outnumbered the other. So I threw the short list away and began to thank God for each and every good quality of my husband. Before I'd finished I felt a new love beginning to kindle. I had added the right fuel to a lukewarm heart.

That night when he came home, I had something to talk about—but not to gain his attention this time.

"Honey, I really love you for just the man you are. Please don't ever change." Gulp—and I meant it.

Boy, did I ever have his attention! He took me in his arms and I melted as his dark brown eyes held mine. "I love you, too," he whispered, "just the way you are."

The sparks began to fly that night and our marriage has grown progressively warmer every day, sometimes igniting to a red-hot flame. (I always did think it would be romantic to have a bedroom fireplace.) And I just keep adding fuel daily. It's as simple as A, B, C.

A: *Accept him as he is.* I don't try to change him anymore. He'll never change anyway, so why bat my head against him and cause him to resent me? He's not perfect but neither am I, and I accept that (about both of us).

He still doesn't waste words, but that's okay with me. He shows me in many other ways that he loves me—a look, a touch, a surprise night out. If he's cross and impatient with me, I just try to remember that he has a right to express his anger; and, in accepting

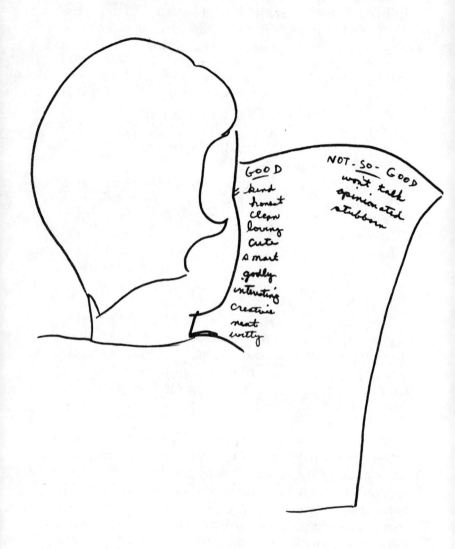

I made a list of his good points and his not-so-good points.

him, I can overlook his actions. This one thing has given him, and me, the freedom to be ourselves.

B: *Believe in him.* We don't always agree on a certain course of action. I know I'm right, and he knows he's right. So what should I do? Believe in him. If he makes a mistake, at least it'll be his mistake. I'll just believe in him. He's doing what he thinks is right, and I'll stand behind him in his decision—and usually he *is* right. But occasionally when he's wrong I'm careful not to say, "I told you so." That's not love. And he may even come to me, confident in my belief in him and say, "I was wrong."

C: *Commit myself to him.* This isn't the kind of commitment involved in a prison term or an insane asylum, but rather the commitment I have to a philosophy or an ideal. I'll stick with him whatever comes, whoever interferes and whenever he needs me. My joy is to make him happy. And I'm learning more each day what brings a sparkle to his eyes and a spring to his step. Am I the loser? No way. God knew what He was doing when He gave us Ephesians five.

These same ABC's are used to enter God's family through the new birth, except that Jesus Christ is the One to accept, believe in and commit myself to. It doesn't surprise me that a wife should respond to her husband in the same way a believer does to Christ, because both the Old and New Testaments compare the husband-wife relationship with that greater spiritual marriage between Christ and His church.

Marriage was given by God to show the world the delights of the union between Christ and the church.

Perhaps in the past my marriage has been a weak portrayal of Heaven and has discouraged some who would otherwise have asked, "What must I do to be saved?"

But there have been some changes made and today I'm not only a happier wife, but my husband is a happier man. I trust that the bedroom in my back forty temple will be a truer expression of the joys of Heaven than my south forty ever was.

Pass the matches, please.

16

Hanging in There

Well, what do you know? Here's that skirt I was going to shorten, and now the length is just right. And here's my green sweater that's been missing for so long. Oh, I'd forgotten all about this bag of mending. And what's this? Some trophies my oldest son won on the track team (how many years ago?).

It had been such a long time since I'd cleaned my closet that I ended up with three bags full—
One for the Goodwill
One for the mission
And one for the trash can
In the kitchen.

It's easy to stuff things in the closet that I don't want to throw away or don't know where else to hide, but there's a limit. My closet seems to catch everything—unfinished needlepoint, used patterns, yardage scraps and mending by the ton.

If only I'd learned that lesson my mother tried so hard to teach me, "A place for everything and everything in its place." (Maybe I would have if she'd learned it from *her* mother!) But it's never too late to start, and I'll try to keep my back forty closet more orderly from now on.

I hope Jesus didn't mean that I should literally shut myself up in the closet when He said, "But thou, when thou prayest, enter into thy closet . . ." (Matthew 6:6), because I could never get into mine.

And besides, I'm ashamed to admit that my quiet time "closet" has been as cluttered and disorderly as the closet in my bedroom. I had planned to mend those torn relationships *one day,* and I really intended to follow God's pattern for the robes of righteousness and also get rid of those trophies of my old nature. So what better time to clean out my spiritual closet than *now,* and to dedicate my back forty closet to communion with God? I know that, to continue building a temple for the Lord, I have to hang in there and not give up. That means I'm going to need the fortification found only in the quiet place (closet) of prayer.

Prayer. What is it? How can my prayer life become more meaningful to me, more effective for others and more honoring to God?

I remember a little song we used to sing in Good News Club called, "Jesus and Others and You." The song pointed out that putting *J*esus first, *O*thers second, and *Y*ourself last was the way to spell J-O-Y. No wonder my prayer closet was a mess. I didn't even know how to spell. What's a Y-O-J anyway?

Colossians 1:18 says of Jesus Christ, "And he is the head of the body, the church: who is the beginning, the firstborn from the dead; that in all things he might have the preeminence"—that is, second to none, unequaled, unrivaled, first place. I hadn't given Him the preeminence, even though my plans for the back forty years were to honor Him.

I had tried to be more pleasing to Him, but was He

I hope Jesus didn't mean that I should literally
shut myself in the closet when I pray.

more pleasing to me? Did I look forward to meeting Him in my quiet time to tell Him of my love? As I read the Bible, was my primary purpose to know Him better and love Him more?

I could see that I needed to reevaluate my Bible study and change my goals. I found Scriptures proclaiming God to be jealous of other allegiances (Exodus 20:5); of His desire to reveal Himself (Proverbs 8:17); and of His pleasure in my worship (I Chronicles 16:29). His will is that I know and love Him. And tell Him so.

This was new to me. Bowing before Him and proclaiming my love. Speaking to Him as a bride does to her husband, admiring Him, adoring Him. But that's what He wants. *LOVE.*

When Jesus Christ has first place in the closet, He will also have first place in the rest of the house. Priorities are seen in their proper perspective. Petty grievances lose their importance, and people become more precious when God is all in all (I Corinthians 15:28).

I soon acquired a greater concern and love for others. And instead of my past critical whine to God about their behavior, I began to pray creatively. God wanted to bless them. He wanted to reveal Himself to them. He wanted them to enjoy worshipping Him. Recognizing His love and concern gave me a better insight into the problems and suffering of my fellow believers. And not only that, I began to see that those who were going their own way were truly loved by God, too.

Jesus' prayer to His Father was that we may be with Him where He is, and that we may behold His glory (John 17:24). Shouldn't this also be my desire for others? I Timothy 2:1,2 instructs me how to pray,

"I exhort therefore, that, first of all, supplications, prayers, intercessions, and giving of thanks, be made for all men; for kings, and for all that are in authority . . . ."

I couldn't pray for all these at one kneeling so I decided to have a prayer list, praying for certain ones each day of the week. Some may feel that a prayer list is too structured, but I found that if I depended solely on spontaneity in prayer or housecleaning, neither would get done.

My back forty closet was becoming more orderly. *J*esus and *O*thers and—*You.*

My own problems seemed smaller with God in the preeminent place. I wasn't falling apart as quickly and found my grocery bill in facial tissues greatly reduced. Nothing could touch me except as my loving Heavenly Father stepped aside and let it through; and He had promised that, "There hath no temptation taken you but such as is common to man: but God is faithful, who will not suffer you to be tempted above that ye are able; but will with the temptation also make a way to escape, that ye may be able to bear it" (I Corinthians 10:13).

Life makes more sense now. And it's possible to do more than just hang in there (by the skin of my teeth). I can hang loose because Jesus is Lord. Lord of my back forty closet.

17

Brightening My Corner

"But I need an outside interest," I grumbled, following my husband to the garage, "'cause all I do is cook meals and clean house."

"That's okay; get one," he answered before slamming the car door, "but I don't want my wife working!"

Hmmm, what did he think cooking and cleaning was? A game of Chinese Checkers with missing marbles? We'd had this same conversation (?) many times. Not that I wanted to get a job—I just felt I needed to do something different. Something to affect those living on the periphery of my back forty, and something just for me.

That night when my husband came home, he was grinning from ear to cheek (I love that crooked smile). "Honey, I've been thinking about what you said this morning, about an outside interest. Come on out and see what I've bought for you."

My pounding heart fluttered to a fl-ump as I looked at my "outside interest"—a brand new easy-start power mower. That wasn't exactly what I had in mind.

Several interesting projects have opened up to me

I looked at my husband's idea of my new "outside interest." That wasn't exactly what I had in mind.

in the last few years. In fact, they were my husband's hobbies and I planned to catch on to his shirttail and learn right along with him.

Photography was the first, but he wasn't too cooperative in the darkroom. We had to set up trays and enlargers in our smaller-than-average bathroom, and only one night of assisting was enough for me. He was so negative! How could I have known I was allergic to developing solution and would sneeze on the strips of drying film? I tried to stifle it, but lost my balance and stepped in the pan of fixer on the floor. The last straw was when he hollered at me for turning on the light. I was only going to get a towel and wipe up the mess.

Then I took golf lessons, and energetically putted toward the day when we would play our first game together. I still don't know why the club slipped out of my hands on the backswing. Besides—he shouldn't have been standing so close.

I knew I would do better at woodworking. *I had to.* I waited until I had read several of his books on cabinetmaking before I displayed my newfound talent. I decided to surprise him with my expertise by staining the top of the end table he was building for his mother. The pieces of rosewood were perfectly matched and sanded to a glassy smoothness. I knew he'd be glad to save some time because he'd already spent over a month on that little table, and I'd be glad to lend some help. After all, I'm to be a helpmeet, aren't I?

I found a small can labelled, "Spanish Walnut Stain," in his workbench. There were other cans, too—cherry stain and maple. I wondered which one he had decided upon.

"Eeney, meeny, miney, moe." The Spanish Walnut

won out. I glopped it on with a brush, then rubbed the excess off with a soft rag. It sure was dark. In fact, it was black! I don't think that was the color he had chosen.

The directions said it was a water base stain, so I washed and scrubbed it with soap and water. The grain just fuzzed up and darkened. Oh, dear. Maybe a little steel wool would smooth it out, but all I could find was an old S O S pad. I scrubbed and sweated. I must have done something wrong.

And to top it off, my poor husband took sick that very night and couldn't even eat his dinner. He did manage to croak before pulling the blankets over his head, "Get your own hobby—*PLEASE!*"

I guess I just can't keep up with my hobby hubby. So I took his advice. I tried volunteer hospital work, but found it too depressing. I never could balance the cash drawer in the hospital gift shop.

Then I took classes at the local junior college, but embarrassed my daughter when I showed up in bobby sox and saddle oxfords.

I even tried leading a group of Campfire Girls, but the forest ranger suggested I quit while I was ahead. (It was only a little fire.) Was there anything I *could* do right? I'd dabbled in oils, but who wants to hang a dabble? I'd attempted to join the church choir, but after auditioning, was asked to take the "very important ministry" of cataloging the music.

There weren't many other doors open to me, at least doors that led to the corner I hoped to brighten. I'd tried hobbies, volunteer work and the arts. As I wrote down my frustrations in my daily journal, I suddenly realized that I really liked to write, although I had never thought of it as a "thing" I could do.

So I applied the knowledge I'd gained from various English classes, the techniques set down by creative writing books (there are shelves of them in the public library), and the simple, clear style propounded by Rudolph Flesch. I enrolled in an evening creative writing class, procured a second-hand electric typewriter, set up a makeshift desk in the corner of my bedroom and, presto!—a writer.

I wrote and wrote and rewrote. I wrote about what I knew. My family, my God. I sold my first article to a Christian magazine six months after setting up my corner office. Oh, joy, I had found my corner brightener. One year later, I had sold two more articles. Slow, but sure. My family was beginning to see me in a new light. I was beginning to see *me* in a new light. Another year went by. I sold my first book!

A whole new future was opening up—speaking engagements, newspaper articles, autographing parties. Could this be happening to me? *Me?* An ordinary-over-the-hill-housewife? "For it is God which worketh in you both to will and to do of his good pleasure" (Philippians 2:13).

How thrilling that He had given me not only an "outside interest," but also a way to serve Him that I enjoyed. And I had always thought "service" was something you did because you had to, something uncomfortable.

Of course, what's exciting to me may be drudgery to you. We each have our own interests and abilities and, committed to Christ, they can benefit more than our own personal need for an outlet.

As I think about my future, it looks brighter every day. In fact, I see so many ideas and stories lurking in the corners of my mind that I wonder if I'll have room on my back forty to finish them all.

18

Washing
the Windows

"Why is it so dark in here? my husband asked one sunny afternoon. "Let's open the drapes!"

"Oh, no," I yelped, grabbing the white, plastic pull from his hand. "It's much cosier with the drapes shut. Anyway, the sun might fade my new paint job."

As I turned away from the window, I heard the swoosh of the drapery rod and a gasp escape my husband's lips. "What on earth—?"

"Well, honey, I planned to tell you about that paint all over the window, but . . ."

Really, I'd tried to get it off with paint thinner and soap and water, and it just spread around until the entire window was an opaque antique white. It gave me the sensation of looking out over a snow covered yard. And that might be real cool on a hot summer day. I kind of liked the idea. But he didn't.

"If you're going to do a job, do it right," he sighed.

I almost answered, "yes, Father." But I knew he had a paint, I mean, a point, and bit my tongue. We both scraped on the window for the next hour and, truthfully, I do prefer green grass in the summertime.

The windows in my back forty temple were spattered and cloudy, too. I'd been careless and lazy about cleanups, and was content to shut the world out and myself in. It was easier to pull the drapes than go through the cleaning process. Besides, when I see clearly through the windows, I can't escape the reality of work that needs to be done, and my responsibility to do it.

"But whoso hath this world's good, and seeth his brother have need, and shutteth up his bowels of compassion from him, how dwelleth the love of God in him" (I John 3:17)?

I'd created the illusion that if I didn't see it, it wasn't my concern. I wonder how many souls have marched past my south forty windows crying for help? And how many slipped into eternity while I hid safely behind my drapes?

Oh, I occasionally peeked out the peephole in my door when I heard approaching steps, but the distorted faraway view left me untouched and often repulsed. I could watch through my peephole undetected and, to the unlovely, I was "out to lunch."

But I would scrape and wash my back forty windows so I could not only view the world clearly, but also reach out with God's love to meet the needs of my brothers and sisters.

I wouldn't mind looking out at the world and then doing my duty (that made me feel noble), but couldn't I at least apply some of that new plastic film to the inside of my windows so that others couldn't see in? I deserve some privacy, don't I? If others look into my life, they'll see my weaknesses and take advantage of me. I'll be too vulnerable.

In the past, it had been important to me that people see only my best side and not know my faults. After all, I wanted to be a "testimony." But James 5:16a says, "Confess your faults one to another, and pray one for another, that ye may be healed." Does that mean that I'm to be so open that I should even confess my faults? But why? ". . . that ye may be healed." I guess hiding behind a mask of self-righteousness is like applying a Band-Aid to a broken arm; complete healing cannot take place until the problem is correctly diagnosed and treated.

Yes, God's temple windows demand a two-way view. I see you and love, and you see me and love. This is the fulfillment of the new commandment that Jesus gave, ". . . that ye love one another; as I have loved you, that ye also love one another" (John 13:34). And how can we truly love each other if we don't really know each other, if we're not open and vulnerable?

Okay, I'm willing to clean my windows, but how? I've tried different products, such as good works sprinkled with liquid self-will. But my efforts, though sincere, only succeeded in making a gloppy mess. What's God's formula?

"Wherewithal shall a young man [middle-age person?] cleanse his way? by taking heed thereto according to thy word. . . . Thy word have I hid in mine heart, that I might not sin against thee" (Psalm 119:9,11).

And Jesus said, "Now ye are clean through the word which I have spoken unto you" (John 15:3).

So I must apply the Word of God to my life, spread it around, let it soak in, then as God reveals my sins, I confess and He cleanses me from all unrighteousness. (I John 1:9).

Talk about powerful detergents! God's Word is power, and I know from previous experience, when I neglect it or read it quickly as a daily duty, my life is weak. And I don't care about others, either. Yes, the Word of God washes me clean, and as a two-edged sword, it also scrapes off the hard, sticky places.

After my windows are clean inside and out, what should I do about the problems I see around me? Should I become involved with those little kids down the street? Must I sit and listen to a dissertation on "the pastor's wife" by a disgruntled church member? Do I have to reach into my own rainy-day pocket when the man across the way is sick and out of work?

To all these questions, I ask, "What would Jesus do?" What did He do when He saw needy children? He reached out in love and refused them not.

How did He respond to the Pharisees and those who were "out of sorts"? He rebuked them firmly with His Word. And He ministered to the poor and needy with kindness, concern, and a few small fishes (Mark 8).

So when I'm in doubt about my ministry to others, I can, through prayer and the Word of God, learn what Jesus would do. As He lives in me by His Holy Spirit, He gives the power to do His will—in every circumstance.

But how about those looking in? Suppose a friend has a complaint against me? Or my husband criticizes something I've tried to do well? Or how about the times my children thoughtlessly take me for granted? Surely I'm justified in drawing my drapes around my hurt and enjoying some good old-fashioned self-pity. If I let them know I'm hurt, they may hurt me more. But if I don't let them know, my wound will fester and not heal.

So, by God's grace, I should take constructive

criticism well and learn from it. Also, when I'm wrongfully accused, I can explain without vindictiveness how those unkind words hurt me. Then Christ can soothe our aching hearts and knit them together in love.

And so it goes—on and on—loving and being loved for as far as I can see through my clean back forty window.

Friend, as long as you're looking in, why not stop and sit a spell?

19

Picking up the Pieces

"Oh, come on, lady, you gotta be kiddin'! I can't lay carpet 'til you get these boards and nails off the floor. I ain't no cleanup man."

Well, of all the nerve! *I* shouldn't have to clean up after the carpenters, and the new carpeting cost enough—why couldn't he do a little extra work? After all, I was in a hurry to decorate and make my house liveable.

That was fifteen years ago when we moved into our new home, and I still remember the expression on the "rugman's" face. Was it amazement or amusement that I would even consider his starting the work before the cleanup was finished? I was premature, I know, but, oh, so eager to get settled. Our first home.

A lot of living has transpired there since that day. Many memories have decorated the walls and lit up the corners, and I occasionally bring them out of the closets of my mind to enjoy. But it's time to redecorate now, and as in those first days when rubbish had to be moved out before we could move in, today in my back forty temple I find I've accumu-

Lady, I can't lay carpet until you get these
boards and nails off the floor!

lated some unnecessary trinkets, baubles and baggage along the way. It's time to pick up the pieces—pieces that someone may stumble over.

"Let us not therefore judge one another any more: but judge this rather, that no man put a stumbling-block or an occasion to fall in his brother's way" (Romans 14:13).

With my drapes wide open and the light streaming in through clean windows, I can clearly see leftover boards and nails scattered across the floor. It's cleanup day—and the most obvious must go first.

I thought, after so many years as a Christian, my life was in pretty good shape. The most glaring forms of worldliness (at least those so specified by my particular brand of Christianity) had been put away. But I found they had been replaced by subtle acts masquerading as "freedom in the Spirit." Could my freedom be someone else's chain?

I almost hate to name some of these "stumbling-blocks," lest I be accused of judging. "Judge not, that ye be not judged" (Matthew 7:1), but I'm commanded to judge myself (I Corinthians 11:31). And if I truly love my fellow Christian, can I allow something in my life that he may fall over?

My own cleanup involves three areas: 1. The church; 2. The world; and 3. The private life.

1. How can my church attendance (or lack of it) influence other Christians? What harm will it do if I miss some of the services? No one will notice. But they do. And a weaker Christian may find my absence just the excuse he needs to stay home on Sunday nights.

And how about my service? I may teach Sunday School and act as a deaconess (for awhile), but what is it to anyone if I don't stay on the job for more than a few months? Suppose I feel led to quit? Am I really led by God—or by my own inconsistency?

"Moreover it is required in stewards, that a man be found faithful" (I Corinthians 4:2). How can I be faithful? Do I have to muster it up? ". . . thy faithfulness reacheth unto the clouds" (Psalm 36:5b).

In the future, I'll depend on God when I feel tired and uninspired, and my dependability in church attendance and Christian service will encourage others to persevere, too.

And how about my attitudes in the church? Am I reverent and attentive to the Word of God? Do I sing the songs with conviction? Am I friendly to the visitors? Do I work with or against the leaders? Am I a purveyor of "gossip" prayer requests?

All of these actions result from attitudes and may be either stumblingblocks or stepping-stones. "Create in me a clean heart, O God; and renew a right spirit within me" (Psalm 51:10).

2. Now I pick up the pieces in an area that leads to "doubtful disputations." What is worldly to one is not to another. Unless an action is specifically mentioned in the Bible as wrong, is it permissible for me to indulge in it? Paul says I'm free and not under bondage, except the bondage of love.

"All things are lawful for me, but all things are not expedient [profitable]: all things are lawful for me, but all things edify not" (I Corinthians 10:23).

There's not much preaching about worldliness these days (probably because there would be a great exodus), but it's a message proclaimed by Paul as the law of expediency; and taken to heart, it could change the whole atmosphere of the church and (surprisingly?) attract unbelievers to a better life.

Are we afraid that teaching good works may confuse the doctrine of salvation by grace alone? But the contrary is true. A life snatched from sin by the grace of God wants to express its love through good works and a pure life. Anyway, that's what happened to me. "... faith without works is dead..." (James 2:26b).

By applying the law of expediency, several things have come to my attention regarding my own worldliness, and I'm sure I'll see more as I grow in the faith. What about the way I dress? Is it modest, becoming to a Christian woman? Or would my clothes cause another to sin?

And how about my eating and drinking? If I talk about the value of nourishing food for good health and weight loss, yet openly (or secretly) habitually consume junk food, I may be putting a stumbling-block in someone's path—or even worse, be disregarding my own convictions (a hypocrite?). Some Christians today, free in the Spirit, are drinking wine (in moderation) with their meals. But would a Christian recently saved from alcoholism be tripped up by such freedom?

And how about my amusements—the places I go, the programs I watch and the books I read? Surely I'm not my brother's keeper here, too. How can I know what is best? I just need to ask myself (and be honest in my answer), "Would Jesus enjoy this? Would it receive His smile of approval? Is it God's best?"

Although many present-day activities are not mentioned in the Bible, there are principles set forth that should help us regarding questionable things.

"And whatsoever ye do in word or deed, do all in the name of the Lord Jesus, giving thanks to God and the Father by him" (Colossians 3:17).

"Let your light so shine before men, that they may see your good works, and glorify your Father which is in Heaven" (Matthew 5:16).

And then, 3. How can my private life—what I am—topple someone on his way to Heaven?

As no one lives unto himself, even moods and expressions affect others. Has your husband ever walked in from work with the burden of the world on his shoulders? Did a big, dark cloud come in with him? Even the children's attitudes about failed tests and broken dates cast a shadow over the household.

But I think this is particularly true of the mother in the home. I seem to set the mood for the entire family. Many times I've seen my children catch my contagious moods, whether depressed or enthusiastic. Humanly speaking, I'm fearful and a worrywart; in Christ, I'm "anxious for nothing." Left to myself, I'm shy and self-conscious; in Him, I'm bold and loving.

Inconsistency and a lack of discipline are products of my nature, too, but as I rely on the indwelling Holy Spirit, I may be ". . . steadfast, unmovable, always abounding in the work of the Lord . . ." (I Corinthians 15:58b).

Am I a Pollyanna to expect so much of myself? I know I'll never be perfect this side of Heaven, but "I can do all things through Christ which strengtheneth me" (Philippians 4:13), so I count on Him to pick up the pieces and dispose of them.

Yes, I want to keep my own back forty house in order, and as my brother's keeper, help him to walk without stumbling. And with those boards and nails out of the way, my Interior Decorator can now begin to beautify His temple.

I wonder what His plans are?

20

Decorating the Interior

I stepped back and admired my outer structure. *Well, it looks great, doesn't it, Lord? The rooms are well planned, too,* I thought. *But something is missing. What is it?*

Look closer, the Lord whispered. *The walls are bare, the floors cold, the windows glare and there's no place to sit and relax. If you like, I'll be your Interior Decorator, too.*

Fantastic! I knew He could decorate the temple so that it would be not only beautiful, but useful.

After recalling some of my past decorating flops, I knew that this time the wisest thing was to turn the entire planning over to the Expert.

One of my problems had always been my compulsive buying sprees. Or, as my husband put it, my "bargain basement bombs." Could I help it if I loved garage sales? You never know when a three-legged desk will come in handy. And some of those pictures might be real antiques. There's that one with the wolf howling on a snowy hillside, and the black velvet copy of Blue Boy—done in green. So what if they don't go with anything? As long as I save money. But my husband doesn't think it's a savings if all my bargains end up in the attic (and neither do I—really).

It's true; I don't have an eye for style or color, and I do want my back forty temple to glorify and honor the Lord, so I'll leave the decorating to Him.

I found in Galatians five a catalog listing of the most popular patterns. They're labeled the "works of the flesh" and the "fruit of the Spirit." Looking over the various pieces of furnishings, I could see that several works of the flesh had prominent places in my old way of life, but I wanted no part of them now. And as the two styles wouldn't mix, there would be no more bargain hunting for me. This time the decorations wouldn't clash but would harmonize perfectly. The fruit of the Spirit would never end up in the attic.

But how could I acquire such beautiful objects and be sure they weren't cheap copies, but the real thing?

The fruit of the Spirit (love, joy, peace, long-suffering, gentleness, goodness, faith, meekness, temperance) is just that—the fruit of the *Spirit*. *I* can't do anything to acquire it, nor can I imitate it. The Holy Spirit does it all. John 15:7,8 says, "If ye abide in me, and my words abide in you, ye shall ask what ye will, and it shall be done unto you. Herein is my Father glorified, that ye bear much fruit . . ."

Much fruit. It sounds wonderful, but how can I know this truth in a practical way? The Bible, though divinely inspired, is practical, and Jesus spoke in a down-to-earth way when He said, "Abide [be at home] in Me . . ." (John 15:4). He was saying that if I find Him to be my place of rest and seek my innermost joy and strength from Him, I am abiding in Him. And only as I keep short accounts with sin, by confessing it and experiencing God's cleansing power, can I continue to abide. (See I John 3:24.)

Is He the Source of my life? Is He the One I live for? Is He the One I'd die for? If my answer to these questions is yes, then I'm abiding in Him. ". . . and my [Jesus'] words abide in you . . ." (John 15:7).

What place does God's Word have in my life? Do His promises come quickly to mind when I'm worried? Do His commands keep me from falling when tempted? Is my heart filled with Scriptural words of praise when I kneel to worship? If so, then His word is abiding in me. So what's the result? Much fruit.

I don't have to "work up" love and perform kind acts. I don't have to emulate joy, and say with a big grin fixed on my face, "Praise the Lord." I don't have to clench my teeth, smooth my brow and try to show peace in the midst of turmoil. That's rotten fruit—it spoils when there is too much heat!

The fruit of the Spirit is a beautiful sovereign act of God in the life of a person who finds Him the All-sufficient One. I don't think one who is Spirit-fruit-decorated is even aware of it. Just as the vine doesn't produce fruit for itself, but for the refreshment of others, so the fruit of the Spirit is not for the enjoyment of the fruitful, but for those who hunger and thirst for God. But even more, the fruit is for the Lord, the Husbandman. He sees it and is pleased.

How can the fruit of the Spirit be manifested in my temple for the Lord?

I see *love* as a mirror, reflecting the person of Jesus. I know I haven't any love of my own, except a selfish love that wants to be loved in return. But the love of God perseveres in all circumstances with never a thought of gain. First Corinthians 13 fully describes this beautiful grace. As my love mirror hangs on the wall of my back forty home, it also reflects the images of those who pass by looking for acceptance and love.

Joy is like a lamp spreading brightness and cheer throughout the life. A lamp isn't as conspicuous in the daylight as it is at night, and joy is more apparent in the dark times of life than when all goes well. What is real joy, but transformed sorrow in the hands of the Saviour?

It's so much more than a happy smile. Today many Christians counterfeit joy. There's a teaching abroad that says, "Smile, no matter what happens." That's not the fruit of the Spirit, but the work of the flesh. Spirit-joy is from within, a sense of quiet gladness in knowing that God is in control no matter how the heart is breaking.

Peace is the next furnishing on the list. And I think of it as it was shown in a story I once read. It seems there was a contest to see who could best paint a picture depicting peace. There were many entries: a pastoral scene, a sunset, a happy family around the table. But the painting that won the prize was a portrayal of a wild ocean storm. The waves pounded against the rocks. The night was dark as heavy clouds pelted icy bullets of rain. Peaceful? Yes, there sleeping in the crevice of a jagged rock was a tiny bird. Protected and warm, it rested, peaceful and oblivious to the storm around it.

That's the picture of peace I want on my wall. Whatever comes, I am in Christ. Nothing can separate me from His love. I can be at peace in Him, my Rock of safety.

Longsuffering is certainly not one of my natural characteristics. Only God could produce such a decoration in my life. To wait and be patient—oh, how I want everything to happen now! That's why I've always used crash diets, painted embroidery and Polaroid pictures. I can't stand to wait. But as I abide in Christ and His words abide in me, He will add this to my temple, too. So I'll sit back in my new chair, longsuffering (it must be a chaise lounge!), and wait. And while I'm waiting, I'll patiently learn the lessons He has for me—a day at a time.

Gentleness: Some people are naturally gentle. Their voices are soft, as is their touch. They move through life serving others in a kind and thoughtful way. But even *they* admit to times when they speak or act harshly. Lasting gentleness is a fruit of the Spirit. And it's not synonymous with Milquetoast, either. A Christian should be strong and persuasive, but temper his remarks with gentleness.

"And the servant of the Lord must not strive; but be gentle unto all men . . ." (II Timothy 2:24). Gentleness soothes as truly as the soft background music of a stereo. And this attribute seems also to fit into the background, calming and soothing, rather than blaring and blasting.

When I think of goodness, I think of a table laden with food (naturally). What is goodness? The opposite of badness, true—but it's also much more. It can't really be described except by studying the Person of God, for when Jesus was once approached as "Good Master," He said, ". . . there is none good but one, that is, God" (Matthew 19:17).

I love that little chorus, "God is so good, God is so good, God is so good, He's so good to me." Simple but beautiful, and a true worship song. And I can share that goodness.

Faith: The theologians say that here (in Galatians 5) this word should be translated faithfulness or perseverance. And, surely, faithfulness is also a fruit of the Spirit. I mentioned this characteristic in "Picking up the Pieces," and realize that if I want to continue serving the Lord, He must supply the faithfulness. And He will, as I abide in Him.

Faithfulness is to "keep on keeping on," day in and day out. I think of it as a good clock, one you can always depend on. I wouldn't want it to be like the one that hangs over my kitchen sink now. It has pointed to five o'clock for the last two years. It only hangs there as a space filler. It's flashy, but not faithful.

Meekness adds the color and fragrance of a bouquet to my back forty temple. And though some may look on meekness as weakness, the Lord Jesus commended it as a strength. "Take my yoke upon you [hard work pulling that plow], and learn of me; for I am meek and lowly in heart: . . ." (Matthew 11:29a). He was submissive to His Father's will, though He was ". . . all the fulness of the Godhead bodily" (Colossians 2:9). And if He, the God-Man, was submissive to His Father, shouldn't I manifest this fruit, too?

Temperance is the thermostat in my home. It sets the temperature and keeps it there. In my south forty years, temperance was only the thermometer and fluctuated constantly. I was hot or cold, depending on my circumstances. But I know now that temperance or moderation in my eating or drinking or whatever I do will bring glory to the Lord. The Holy Spirit will adjust my thermostat to suit Him (not my whims), for He is the Owner of the temple.

Surely such beautiful graces decorating my back forty home will remind others of the presence of Jesus Christ, for it is not I, but Christ who liveth in me (Galatians 2:20).

Unfortunately, with my weakness for bargains, I may foolishly add some old flesh-works now and then, but as I confess my sin to God, He will throw them out and move His decorations back to the prominent place.

Boy, am I glad to be on personal terms with the greatest Interior Decorator in the universe!

21

Occupying
the Premises

I was tired and, well, a little lazy, so I decided to put off the housework and spend the day reading. I sure hoped no one would drop in. The dishes were still in the sink, the beds unmade, and I should go visit my sick mother-in-law. But my husband wouldn't be home from work for hours; I could get everything in shape by then, and I'd call Mom tonight.

So I snuggled down in my chair, feeling sinfully cozy on such an overcast day. It looked like rain. The clouds were so dark and heavy. A perfect day to kick back and indulge myself in Hercule Poirot's last adventure.

What was that rumble? Was it thunder? It sure was getting dark—must be a big storm. I turned on the lights. How strange. Dark as midnight, yet high noon. The rumble grew louder, almost deafening. I put down my book.

Then, without warning, the roof exploded off the house. Trumpets, thunder and roaring crashed over my head. I peeked through the cracks of my fingers to see the black sky rolling back like a scroll. Blinding Light. There He was! Resplendent in His glory and reaching out nail-scarred hands. Jesus!

Feeling a little lazy, I snuggled down in my chair to indulge in Hercule Poirot's last adventure.

I fell to my knees and lifted my arms, "Hallelujah!" My heart pounded as I strained my eyes to take in every part of His lovely face. Darkness.

I touched my eyes to be sure they were open. "Ouch." Then I heard the soft breathing of my sleeping husband next to me. Jesus hadn't come. It was all a dream.

A mixture of disappointment and relief swept over me. Of course, I wanted to see Him—but when I was busy, not sloughing off.

This dream, shortly after my conversion, left a lasting impression on me. The return of Christ so occupied my thoughts those first days as a Christian that I often got up at night to see if He was coming. I lived with the constant awareness of His return. I longed for it. But as the days and years passed, the anticipation of His return withered into a vague yearning.

I haven't been living with the expectation that He may come soon. Today. I know He wants me to eagerly await His return as I live on my back forty, for ". . . every man that hath this hope in him purifieth himself, even as he is pure" (I John 3:3). And I don't want Him to find me idle or backslidden like I was in that dream so many years ago. I want to be serving the Lord. He said in Luke 19:13, ". . . Occupy till I come."

The dictionary defines "occupy" as, "to take possession of; to dwell in; to employ oneself." So if I plan to occupy the premises of my back forty till He comes, there'll be some changes made—today. Plans for a more disciplined and orderly life. Goals for each day, as well as for the future.

"If any of you lack wisdom, let him ask of God, that giveth to all men liberally, and upbraideth not; and it shall be given him" (James 1:5).

Each morning as I bow before the Lord and commit the day to Him, I can ask for wisdom— wisdom to do only those things that He wants me to do, and wisdom to leave undone what isn't in His will for the day.

I have a "Week at a Glance" calendar that I've been using since the first of the year. It's a great help to me to be able to see what I have done, what I am doing, and what I plan to do, all written down in my black book. Each morning after my Bible study and prayer time, I plan my day, listing the things that need to be done. (I give myself time to read and relax, too.) I decide what to fix for dinner, and who I need to cheer up with a card or phone call. Then, as each thing is completed, I check it off. What a morale booster to see all those checks! If I don't finish a job, I write it at the top of the next day's plans. (This gets those unpleasant jobs like cleaning under the sink and taking the wax off the kitchen floor done!)

And I feel differently about my housework now. Instead of complaining about the menial, low-class job of housekeeping, I now see that whatever I'm doing, wherever I am, I can bring glory to the Lord as I watch for His return. The drudgery is gone. I serve the Lord Christ.

I have goals for the future, too—things to learn, books to read, books to write. And as I live one day at a time, I'm making plans for the days and years ahead. One day, if Christ hasn't returned yet, they too will be on my "completed" list.

I'm accomplishing so much these days, and I even have more time for fun. I'm not as uptight as I was on my south forty, and it's all because I've committed the day to Jesus Christ, the coming King. When the day is His, no matter what I'm doing—reading, scrubbing, writing, or playing—I'll be glad to see Him. In fact, once again I'm, anticipating His return.

As in my dream, the days are getting darker and there are storm clouds gathering on the horizon. I hear the rumble of thunder in the distance. It's almost midnight.

"And when these things begin to come to pass, then look up, and lift up your heads; for your redemption draweth nigh" (Luke 21:28).

It can't be long now. The daily newspaper proclaims the distress of nations and men's hearts are failing them for fear. My heart leaps at the thought—maybe today.

The preparations are almost ready. He has gone to prepare a place for us, and the Holy Spirit is preparing us for the place. Each day a new grace is being added to our character so we may be presented without spot and without wrinkle to Him who loved us and died for us.

I'm ready, waiting—and occupying the premises till He comes.

Are you?

"Even so, come, Lord Jesus" (Revelation 22:20b).

22

Adding on Rooms

Several years have passed since I started building on my back forty, and it's time to look over those original blueprints and evaluate the work that's been done. Have I forgotten anything?

The outer structure is holding its own. Oh, occasionally a bulge develops in the siding or a lump appears in the wall, but I'm quick to make repairs before I get out of shape again. It still isn't easy to diet and keep my body in good condition, but then, it keeps me trusting the Lord for His strength in the everyday business of living (and that's good).

There are a few more gray hairs and wrinkles today, but I've accepted them as a natural badge of "wisdom." And why not? I'm not the only one who's growing older, and besides, if I stop aging, I stop living.

The foundation is strong and stedfast, as the Holy Spirit controls and leads me through each day. Once in a while, a shingle slips off the roof and has to be replaced because I don't always remember to thank and praise God for everything. But when I hear the thud of a fallen shingle, I know it's time to stop and see God's plan in every circumstance—and praise Him.

The rooms are intact. Touch-ups and cleaning are frequent so I won't have to completely remodel my temple again. After all, the back forty is all I have left, and I want to make the best of it. The living room, family room and kitchen continue to offer warmth and fellowship to friends and family as they come and go. And, well, that fire in the bedroom still flares up and sheds a warm glow over our marriage.

I especially enjoy my bright corner, as new friends and experiences open up through my writing ministry. I hope to expand my corner to a full room.

"After 'C' is married, maybe I can have a whole room to myself," I said to my husband this summer. "We've always been so crowded with six children in a three bedroom house. It'll be great to have more space."

Yes, another child moved out recently. We spent most of the summer on wedding plans, and her beautiful garden wedding was all we had hoped it would be.

Now she is gone. And I miss her, but... A room. An empty room. (I guess I feel like Thoreau when he wrote, "I would rather sit on a pumpkin and have it all to myself than to be crowded on a velvet cushion.")

Oh, joy. Now I'll have a place to put my books so I can reach them. Under the bed is so awkward. I could spend the day writing in solitude instead of directing traffic wending its way through manuscripts and typewriters to the telephone and bathroom. A room of my own. Could it really be?

I began to plan where I would put my desk (under the window would be nice). I'd have a bookcase here, and a file cabinet there, and oh, my bulletin board would be just perfect right there.

But one evening I heard my husband talking to "K," our oldest daughter. "I realize you're a little hard up right now, so why don't you move in here until you get on your feet?"

"But, Dad," I heard her say, "I don't want to impose on you guys. I've been gone for three years (away at school). It just wouldn't be right."

"Sure," he said, "it'll be fine. We have an extra room. And after you've been teaching awhile and get some money saved, you can move into an apartment of your own."

"Well, okay, thanks."

"Your mother will be so happy. You know how much she loves to have you kids around."

Hmm, that's that. I guess I won't have an office after all. Sure, I love my family and want them nearby, but . . . .

Things don't always work out like we've planned. In fact, I might say, things usually don't work out like we've planned. The Bible puts it well. "Boast not thyself of tomorrow; for thou knowest not what a day may bring forth" (Proverbs 27:1). I'd had my heart set on a room of my own. Oh, I was willing to share it with an occasional overnight guest, but now I would have to wait. (Where's that longsuffering, Lord?) I was disappointed and had to make some adjustments. But isn't that part of life?

This is a training ground, and I'll be in training until the Lord calls me home, so what lesson does He want me to learn from this change in my plans?

Many changes come at this time of life: a relative dies, and their mate moves in; a child's marriage breaks up, and they come home with the baby; a husband is disabled and must stay home day after day. How can I cope with such unplanned events?

I have to get out the blueprints and add on a room. I have to be able to stretch my love and plans to include those whose plans have gone awry, too.

It wasn't my daughter's choice to move in with us. It was a necessity. It wasn't my relative's choice that her husband pass away. It was God's plan. So I can either get "flustrated" (as my friend, Margaret, says) when my blueprint needs adjustments, or I can look to the Lord who knows my wants as well as my needs, and be pliable in His hands.

I know of some friends living on the back forty who've had to add sickrooms as they learned to live with pain, sun porches for the rehabilitation of broken hearts, and laundry rooms to work in after being deserted by their husbands. It hasn't been easy for any of them. But who said life was easy? I read the other day, "The difficulties of life are intended to make us better, not bitter" (author unknown).

Jesus said His yoke was easy and His burden was light, and that yoke symbolizes hard work. Toil and sweat. But sharing the load with Jesus makes life not only bearable, but enjoyable.

I'm sure that my back forty temple will need additions from time to time as I occupy the premises, but I'll live each day for Him, waiting for His return and remodeling as He shows me. "Being confident of this very thing, that He which hath begun a good work in you will perform it until the day of Jesus Christ" (Philippians 1:6).

Then one day I'll move out of this temple into the mansion that He has prepared for me (John 14:2). That's the day I'm looking forward to. Moving day.

Off the back forty and into eternity.

Just think, someday (if Jesus is your Owner and Contractor, too) we'll be neighbors!